Sanctuaries: Parks, Preserves, and Places of Refuge in the World

Mary A. Hood

Published by Spring Crane Press
Dundee, NY

Cover design by Larah Ritchie at MindMeld Creative
Indexed by Catherine Goddard

BISAC: NAT011000

ISBN: 978-1974659746

Library of Congress Control Number: 2017913195
CreateSpace Independent Publishing Platform, North Charleston, SC

Sanctuaries: Parks, Preserves and Refuges of the World
Hood, Mary A 1944
Includes bibliographical references and index
1 Nature Conservation 2. Natural History 3.Travel

Contents

Introduction

The dunes were burnt sienna and stretched barren and endlessly until they reached the edge of the sky. Our guide had hired camels and we were bumping our way across the Tunisian Sahara from our tent camp in Ksar Ghilane Oasis to the ancient fortress of Tisavar. The history of the fortress announced over breakfast had something to do with a military standoff against great odds, but the details were fuzzy and a little hard to comprehend that early in the morning. It may have involved Roman legions against local tribes, or from an earlier time where the enemy was Alexander, or later and the enemy was Germans. Like many deserts, this one had preserved its war-faring history with great efficacy, and Tisavar was a massive military ruins of bleached stone in an empty landscape, preserved by the government of Tunisia as a national historical monument. Unlike the nearby fictional village of Tatouine constructed to make Star War movies, the fortress of Tisavar was a real place, not a wildlife sanctuary exactly but a place preserved as a historical site.

Two hours of camel trekking was enough for me, as the rocking and swaying was nauseating and the intense sun gave me a terrible headache. I couldn't imagine traveling this way every day for months at a time but this is what the local Berbers do to make a living. As we neared the fort, a group of young riders on ATVs came speeding out of nowhere, popping up over a dune and zooming through our caravan. The camels did not like the noise and disruption and let everyone know it by snorting, stomping, bucking and generally misbehaving, giving the drivers and us riders a hard time controlling them. As the kids on the ATVs zoomed by and faded into the dunes, one hollered in a deep southern twang, "Where y'all from?" that universal question strangers and travelers always seem to ask one another. "Where's home?" the question I encounter wherever I go, the one that identifies me, places me in the context of others and makes solid my connection with place.

In many cultures, "home" isn't just where you come from, it's who you are. The significance and importance of place, *home* probably being the most consequential element of place, is clearly a fundamental feature not only of human life but all life. Every creature, every plant, even every microbe has a sense of place and home, a knowing where it can live and thrive. As an ecologist, I have had a long-time interest in the concepts of place, home and habitat. In the context of a wildlife refuge or preserve, place or habitat for humans and place or habitat for other creatures have been thought of as adversarial. The very nature of a refuge suggests a place that excludes humans because human activity has resulted in the demise of other species or at the very least led to their detriment. I began traveling the world to visit protected lands in order to see if refuges could effectively protect vulnerable species without the exclusion of humans and to see if refuges were really making a difference in maintaining earth's biological diversity.

The World Database on Protected Areas (WDPA), a joint effort between the United Nations Environmental Programme World Conservation Monitoring Center (UNEP-WCMC), the International Union for Conservation of Nature (IUCN), and the World Commission on Protected Areas (WCPA), estimate that there are 161,000 protected areas (as of October 2010) representing 10 to 15 percent of the world's land mass. E. O. Wilson in *Half Earth: Our Planet's Fight for Life* (2017) has proposed a goal of one-half of earth's land mass set aside for conservation. While a laudable target, most conservationists are probably more realistic with modest proposals of around 25 percent of the earth's landmass as a more doable goal.

The folks responsible for such conservation efforts range from professional conservationists trained in biology, ecology, and management to concerned citizens with little or no scientific background. Paul Hawken in *Blessed Unrest: How the Largest Movement in the World Came into Being and Why No One Saw It Coming* (2007) estimates there are over a million organizations whose mission is to save earth's biological heritage, not to mention the undocumented individual efforts of millions of ordinary folks who are re-wilding their backyards and preserving borders and edgelands.

The categories of protected lands chronicled here have many designations: nature preserves, bird sanctuaries, wildlife refuges, wilderness areas, national parks, local parks and preserves, natural monuments, habitat or species management areas, and natural areas where sustainable use of natural resources has been made the rule. Described here are over sixty different refuges in twenty different countries. Woven into these visits are the many elements of sanctuary: safety, protection, rescue, freedom from exploitation and abandonment, as well as the qualities of the sacred and the sublime. Each preserve reflects a narrative about something we value, and out of that concern, places of safety have been created. Collectively, these parks and preserves give tangible affirmations of our efforts to save endangered animals, protect rare plants, keep lands free of development and industrial devastation, and keep our spaces green, wild, open, and as "natural" as possible.

Rio Electrico in Argentina's Los Glaciers National Park begins with an exploration of why we write about the places we love. By interweaving sites along the Platte River that protect the sandhill cranes with accounts from iconic American writers of the Midwest, the second chapter illustrates how place and landscape play an important role in our literature. The chapter on the Eufaula National Wildlife Refuge describes a dammed river and an encounter with an endangered species that makes its home in the southern U.S. wetlands. And finally in the geological category of rivers, remote northeast India offers refuges near tributaries of the Brahmaputra (in the Himalayans) and several along the floodplain of the Brahmaputra.

Amelia Island, a barrier island off the east coast of Florida, exemplifies the tension between preservation and development or sprawl. In the Chihuahuan Desert, the Sky Islands present the conservation of the unique flora of the southwest with tales of Davis Mountains, a million Mexican free-tail bats leaving Carlsbad Caverns, and the hoodoos of the Chiricahua National Monument.

International preserves include a variety of well-known and lesser-known parks and protected areas. Traveling the Ring Road in Iceland, birding the Mindo cloud forest in Ecuador, turtling the Galapagos, colliding with brown bears in the Carpathian Mountains of Romania, spotting the Abyssinian wolf in the Bale Mountains of Ethiopia, searching for flamingos in the Argentinean Andes, I encountered numerous endangered or threatened species in these places. In Tunisia the flamingos of Djerba illustrate a protected species whose sanctuary is without explicit borders. In the Baja California Peninsula, gray whales and frigate birds add to encounters with the rare creatures of desert coastal ecosystems. Mexico's west coast with its mangrove swamps, and Norway and Finland's taiga, tundra, and fjords provide landscapes of astounding beauty and offer sanctuary to a diversity of wetland tropical and arctic birds. Mayan ruins and fincas of Guatemala reflect some of the best conservation efforts of Central America, while Colombia's El Paujil Bird Reserve offers one of the finest models of a South American bird sanctuary. The African countries of Namibia, Botswana, and Zambia reveal protected lands that provide habitat to endangered and threatened animals sustained by funds from tourism.

The final chapter sums up some of the concepts that are being used by today's modern professional conservationists, how inclusion conservation seems to be working, how funding and support varies, and how diverse the many ways folks have invented to protect the lands they care about. From the ocotillo of the Chihuahuan Desert to the orchids of Patagonia, from the Andean flamingos to the African flamingos of Tunisia, from the grasslands of the U.S. Midwest to the glaciers of South America, these refuges serve as witness to the beauty and efficacy of protected lands. By witnessing these places, it is my hope that the value of protected lands will be reaffirmed and result in continual momentum to help keep them places of true sanctuary. Join me now as we visit some of the world's well-known and not-so-well-known sanctuaries.

RIVERS

CHAPTER 1.

Río Eléctrico, Writing the River: Argentina, Los Glaciers National Park

The plan was to hike the river trail four miles to a base camp known as Piedra del Fraile, or the Friary Stone, which serves as the gathering place for climbers going on to the Patagonian glacier fields, have lunch and walk back. The day was sunny and cool, and the sky was smooth as porcelain, Delft blue etched with white, lenticular clouds. Wind-sheared clouds the shape of flying saucers, melon bowls, and a stack of pancakes, with a black speck of a condor gliding among them mosaicked the sky. In the distance the peaks of Cerro Chaltén were haloed in a thin veil, forming a high rim to the landscape. Chaltén, whose name is an aboriginal Tehuelche word meaning "smoking mountain," always has a cloud or two caught in its 11,000-foot peaks. The mountain's reputation for being one of the most difficult to climb because of its sheer granite cliffs and treacherous weather seemed well deserved.

Smooth white river stones covered the ground and sparkled with reflected sunlight. Large chalky boulders etched with black crusty lichens marked the trail in fleur-de-lis, and Chilean swallows darted above the river like tiny boomerangs scooping up insects. When we entered the shade of the forest, the temperature dropped ten degrees. The forest canopy was not high, maybe twenty feet, and the trees were knotty and gnarly. They were lenga or southern beech (*Nothofagus pumilio*) probably two to five hundred years old, according to our guide, Paola. The understory was open and grassy, but the ground was littered with fallen limbs and broken trunks from the many Antarctic storms. The old trees and fallen branches gave the forest a whimsical, spooky look. It could have been a place where gnomes and goblins might come to life on a moonlit night and dance the night away.

Dead branches still clung to the trees and many trees had only partial crowns. Heavily impacted not only by blowdowns but fire, insects, fungi, and grazing animals, the trees had the scraggly look of hard-times survivors. Because lenga wood does not decompose rapidly in the cold Patagonian climate, the tree remains scattered about the forest floor would stay there for a long time. While the defining trees of this Magellanic deciduous forest are the lengas, patches of nire trees (of the related species *N. antarctica*) also grew, mostly around the periphery, and not much taller than shrubbery.

Lengas are indigenous only to the cold, dry, subalpine slopes of the southern Andes, and it is these trees and their interrelationships with the other species that make the ecology of these southern forests so intriguing (Veblen et al., 1996). They grow at altitudes of sea level to around 6,000 feet. At sea level they reach forty to fifty feet but are shrub-sized at highest altitudes. Here along the Río Eléctrico at 3,000 feet, they were about mid-sized. Trees in the genus *Nothofagus* (about thirty five species) are ancient, having evolved eighty million years ago when the earth's land was a single collective mass. Found today only in Australia, New Zealand, Tasmania, New Guinea, New Caledonia, and the southern part of South America, they are living fossils of the primal mega-continent known as Gondwana.

The bark of the lenga trees was deeply pitted and grooved like the wrinkled face of a tribal elder. Thumb-sized leaves, dark green, tough and stiff, with fine-toothed edges, smelled tangy when crushed. Paola told us that in April (fall in the southern hemisphere), they turn the color of red maples. Last year when she was walking the trail, she thought the forest was on fire. The wood has a warm crimson hue, and as timber it is known as fireland cherry. The trees are wind pollinated, having evolved before pollinating insects were even a gleam in nature's eye.

The branches of the lengas were adorned with epiphytes, residents that depend upon both the nutrients and the solidity of the old trees. Like accessories, they looked decorative but these plants are far more functional than ornamental. They are an integral part of the complex ecology of the Andean beech forests. One parasitic plant known as Chinese lantern (*Myzodendrum* species) has the same relationship to its tree host as mistletoe. In various stages of growth, green (growing), white (flowering), and rust colored (acquiescence), the forest resembled a garlanded dance hall strewn with crepe-paper flowers. Another epiphyte, a lichen known as old man's beard (*Usnea* species), formed tufts of green-gray fuzz that hung from the trunks of the old trees like lint. Yet another lichen (*Protousnea* species) draped down like long flowing scarves. Biologically, these hangers-on are crucial in the cycling of water, minerals, and carbon.

Below the canopy in the grassy understory where shafts of light stretched down like white streamers, a garden of wildflowers bloomed: patches of Magellanic pea (*Lathyrus magellanicus*), sea pink (*Armeria maritima*), yellow and purple violets (*Viola* species), and the bright yellow socks of lady slippers (*Calceolaria uniflora*). A club moss (*Lycopodium magellanicum*) formed the background of the forest floor and colored it avocado green.

Where the trail made a graceful curve toward the river, a fallen tree trunk marked the shady home of three species of orchids. The porcelain orchid (*Chloraea magellanica*) in full green-veined bloom was an exquisite ceramic. The prima donna of the understory opera, it was the star attraction. With its cryptic fungal associates working below ground and its contrived sex-appealing flower aboveground attracting insects, the plant was irresistible on so many levels. The dog orchid (*Codonorchis lessonii*) growing in bright clusters was a white-robed chorus, and the yellow orchid (*Gavilea lutea*), a week past its prime, could have been a wilted, aging diva.

The trail sloped upward, and the river changed from a quiet stream to a raging surge. The churning waters grew louder and turned the color of chum. Paola called it "glacier-melt-in-a-hurry gray." When we arrived at Friary Stone camp, we spread our sack lunches on a wooden table at the river's edge and gulped down our sandwiches to the river's percussion. The air vibrated with resistance, stone resisting water, water resisting stone, splashing, rattling, crashing, hammering its way over and down, around boulders, waters determined to reach lower ground.

We rested a while and listened to a story one of our hiking companions told. The woman was in her mid-sixties, trim and fit, with a slight limp. She used two walking sticks. She and her husband had been hiking some years back in the Rockies. Their guide had led them onto a steep trail covered in loose stones. The trail bent around a boulder and opened onto a slope that plunged hundreds of feet down into a deep canyon. The first few yards were all right, she said, but as she moved forward, the stones began to slip and she lost her footing. She thought she was going to slide right off that mountain. Trying to regain her footing by digging in as hard as she could with the toe of her boots, she discovered she then couldn't move. She was stuck. Every attempt she made to move resulted in more sliding. She hung onto that tenuous spot for what seemed hours. By inching her way with the help of her walking sticks back to solid ground, she finally hit hard trail.

Exhausted, she sat on the ground shaking and wondering how

she had made it. The guide came bouncing up and asked if she was OK. He admitted his choice of trails was probably a bit risky, but wasn't it exciting? She was so furious with that foolish, short-sighted boy who would risk her life for his adventure, she could have pushed him off the mountain.

After packing the remains of our lunch we began the trek back. Overhead, the chatter of a pair of austral parakeets filled the air. What odd music, the squawks of parakeets. What could be more atypical in a high glacial zone than tropical birdsong? In the small clearing, the pair could be seen slipping in and out of their nesting hole in an old lenga tree. The tree seemed to be opening its branches like welcoming arms about to embrace the huge green birds.

Further down the trail in the top of another lenga, a Chilean flicker repeated its three-note call: "Pi –*ti* -o, Pi –*ti* -o." The bird's name, pitio woodpecker, comes from its call, a cry that reminded me of those wanton notes from the song "Maria" from *West Side Story*. But the most exciting sound was the dry rapping, the double tap, tap, of the Magellanic woodpecker. A sudden movement to our left and the huge dark bird flew right in front of us across the trail. As it zoomed through the branches and disappeared far back into the forest, we caught only a brief glimpse. For such an enormous bird—it's about the size of a pileated woodpecker with a red head and black body—we were surprised its movements were so quick and its appearance so momentary.

Delaying the end of our trek for as long as possible, we dallied at the river's edge, scanning the rocks, beachcombing the river's debris. (Can a river have a wrack line?) Paola talked about seeing a group of huemul deer on her hike the week before. She recalled how they blended in with the landscape so well she almost missed them. And then she told of two guides who saw a puma not far from where she spotted the deer. I thought how universal is our need to recall the animals we see and to tell others of their presence. Like children taking joy in the naming of the animals from favorite storybooks, it seems we adults need to tell of our encounters with animals as well.

What is it about this river that makes me need to write it? Is writing the river an attempt to give it value, and if I write the river, call the plants and animals by their names, put them in my best words, will the words bear witness to its richness? Certainly, the rare creatures and the dramatic landscape that have been part of the river for millions of years, like all beautiful things, inspire writing. But it might be more than that. Perhaps if I can write the river well enough, others will know its value and be moved to keep it safe.

Over the mountain fifty miles north of the park, the Pascura and the Baker Rivers may not be as safe. HidroAysen, the Chilean-European utility company, planned to dam the rivers, build six hydroelectric plants, and construct a one thousand five hundred-mile corridor of power lines and towers (one of the longest clear-cuts in the world) to transport electricity to Santiago (International Rivers, 2009). The electricity was not designed to be used for individual homes but would power heavy industry and mining activities. HidroAysen's environmental impact study revealed thousands of serious flaws and ignored seismic and hydrological risks and potential flooding of San Rafael National Park. The impact on the flora and fauna of the region would be devastating. On January 29, 2012, the $7 billion project was approved by commissioners appointed by President Sebastian Pinera, but because of huge protests from environmental groups the project was put on hold. Whether the hold is temporary is uncertain. As of 2016, the Chilean government has rejected permits to build the dams, but nothing in politics is ever certain.

Because Los Glaciers National Park is a UNESCO World Heritage Site, it is protected. By preserving these lands as a park, the people of Argentina and the world are saying "this is a place we cherish; this is a place that must be kept as it is; a place you may visit, you may have your adventures here, you may find beauty or inspiration, but you cannot log, you cannot build here, you cannot dam the rivers, you cannot clear cut, you cannot destroy any part of it. You may visit and then you must leave. You may not be foolish and short-sighted here."

There are places in the world that must be cherished and kept undisturbed—would that we could protect them all. Would that we could do this to the whole earth. Would that our governments would listen to those who say these places are invaluable. Would that every dam builder, every tree cutter, could listen to the river and know it as the lengas and the Magellanic woodpeckers know the river, as home.

CHAPTER 2.

A Place of Cranes: United States, Nebraska, The Platte River

The thirty-something waitress who served us breakfast at the Howard Johnson in Grand Island had a brush cut, a tight-fitting blouse, and a skimpy skirt. The restaurant was dark and dimly lit as a barroom. When she noticed our binoculars, she asked where we were from. We said New York—we were here to see the cranes. She explained, "Well, I don't know, but every time the cranes come, my calves get sick." When she brought out plates of greasy scrambled eggs, soggy toast, and partially cooked bacon, she further remarked, "We'll probably be the first ones in the country to be wiped out by the bird flu."

The following morning, we ate at Harriet's Cafe in the small town of Dannebrog. Harriet's Cafe was her home, and the walls were full of pictures of friends and plaques with down-home humor like "Dinner Choices: 1. Take it or 2. Leave it." Cross-stitch samplers offered birds and flowers, and words like "love" and "friendship" were embroidered in red and blue thread. A woman in her 80s, Harriet was tall and agile. She greeted us with a smile and friendly chatter, pointing out her ancient stove and some of her treasured knickknacks. When she noticed our binoculars, she went out back, retrieved a pair of bronze cranes and set them on the tables "to make you feel more welcome," she said. The oatmeal, full of plump raisins, and the Danish pancakes, thin and chewy, were scrumptious. While we wolfed down our breakfast, she walked across the street to the grocery store and returned with a fresh chicken that she cut up, battered in flour, put into a big skillet, and began to pan fry. I asked my traveling companions if we might stay for lunch.

How different these two women were. They could have been characters from two of the novels I had been reading. I try to read novels, essays, or travelogues about a place before visiting to get a feel for the region. The waitress at the Howard Johnson could have been a character from *The Echo Maker* while Harriet might have stepped out of *My Antonia*. Willa Cather's (1918) *My Antonia*, published so many years ago, celebrates the American pioneer, the frontier, the immigrant, and the heartland. Idealizing the virtues of independence, hard work, and asceticism, the book interweaves characters and the land in such a way that the prairie serves not only as setting, but as an essential element of the story. Descriptions such as "blustery winters with little snow, when the whole country is stripped bare and gray as sheet-iron" create a landscape against which the characters struggle to survive. *The Echo Maker* (Powers 2006) published a hundred years later and awarded the 2006 National Book Award, also contains extraordinarily beautiful descriptions. For example, the book opens with these lines:

> *Cranes keep landing as night falls. Ribbons of them roll down, slack against the sky. They float in from all compass points, in kettles of a dozen, dropping with the dusk. Scores of Grus canadensis settle on the thawing river. They gather on the island flats, grazing, beating their wings, trumpeting: the advance wave of a mass evacuation. More birds land by the minute, the air red with calls... The sky, ice blue through the encroaching willows and cottonwoods, flares up, a brief rose, before collapsing to indigo.*

The book ends with these lines:

The outcome of owls will orchestrate the night, millions of years after people work their own end. Nothing will miss us...cranes or something like them will trace rivers again. When all else goes, the birds will find water.

Beautiful descriptions, certainly, but the events of the novel, an accident leaving an irresponsible young man brain damaged with a rare perceptional disorder, are not beautiful, and the characters are dysfunctional and alienated. The gorgeous setting stands separate from the characters and their actions. Perhaps it was the author's intent to portray what he believes we have become, a species deeply disconnected, alienated from our land, the natural world, and each other. The author's attempts to present such ideas are certainly worthwhile, but I sometimes wonder how so many of our modern fiction writers can bear to create such dismal characters and to live with them day after day.

The Platte River joins the Missouri River near Omaha, and with our guide, Mark Suomala, we decided to explore the area before heading out to Grand Island. A drive through Omaha, through the downtown, and then along the freeways to the surroundings brought to mind the descriptions of Robert Vivian in *Cold Snap as Yearning* (Vivian 2001). In an essay called "The Tides, The Tides" he writes of his hometown, "sky blazing...drop dead boredom in an insurance office, where your cubicle is like everyone else's...Omaha is not a great city, in the sense of grandeur or history; it sits on the muddy Missouri like a car battery waiting to be sold, barely used, clean and dirty in equal amounts (shiny cover, soiled underparts), functional but woebegone outside the belly of its never-car" (Vivian 2001: 91, 97). Vivian sees the homeless, the downtrodden, the desperate, and yet he loves his hometown because it is "the savage place in my heart and the gentle corner" (Vivian 2001: 100). With his keen eye and skillful prose, he offers his home in beautiful lyrical language, language that gives hope that there is both enjoyment and meaning in living even if it is in the drabbest, flattest land of mid America.

On the eastern shore of the Missouri, the Loess Hills run north and south for nearly one hundred and twenty miles. Only a few miles wide, their rounded domes look like sand dunes, and they are actually dunes. Clay dunes, blown in by ancient Pleistocene winds, they once undulated with tall prairie grasses. Today they grow trees. The handsome young ranger at the Hitchcock Nature Center explained how he and his staff were trying a new approach to prairie restoration, eradicating the trees and bringing back the original prairie grasses using fire. By controlled burning, the trees, which drain too much water from the soil, could be eliminated, and the grasses would grow back. It would take time but the native prairie could be restored, and what was so encouraging, he claimed, was that the local land-owners wholeheartedly supported the restoration efforts. Of course, systematic prairie restoration is not really a new phenomenon in Nebraska. It has been going on for some years. Bill Whitney of Aurora, Nebraska, began studying the prairie, harvesting prairie grass seed and conducting prairie restoration experiments as early as the 1970s. Since then, native prairie lands have been restored by both conservation organizations and individual efforts.

Located on an old oxbow of the Missouri, the De Soto National Wildlife Refuge provided a floodplain forest and Harris's sparrows. Black-bibbed, pink-billed, the birds resembled house sparrows with pizzazz. They buzzed about in the thickets while our guide Mark reviewed for us their field marks. After wintering in the Great Plains, the birds would be migrating soon to breed in the boreal forest-tundra of northern Canada. Christopher Norment, who spent several summers studying the ecology of Harris's sparrows in this wilderness, writes of his explorations in *Return to Warden's Grove: Science, Desire, and the Lives of Sparrows* (Norment 2008: 4). "Whatever meaning I can gather from my experiences there (on the harsh Canadian tundra) lies with the Harris's Sparrows, the process by which I learned something about their lives, and the land that enveloped both the animals and me." In the blending of the scientific and the poetic, the sparrow and its environment, he attempts in his lovely prose to discover a more inclusive view of the world and our place in it.

At the visitor center, we walked through an exhibit of the recovered steamboat, *Bertrand*, and marveled at the rows of excavated goods. Thousands of bottles lined the shelves like tiny tin toy soldiers, dark flasks holding mercury used in mining, tools such as hammers and chisels, clothes and even luxury items like bottles of olive oil, mustard from France, bitters, canned peaches, and brandied cherries. The plaques explained that during the 19th and early 20th centuries, more than four hundred steamboats sank or were stranded between St. Louis, Missouri, and Ft. Benton, Montana. The *Bertrand* sank in 1865, sixty years after the expeditions of Lewis and Clark. So the exhibit was a reminder of how quickly we Americans moved into the West bringing our consumer habits with us.

South of Omaha, near the confluence of the Platte and the Missouri, the Fontenelle Forest rises from the floodplain. With steep hills and a high canopy, the forest preserve has a nature center and sixteen miles of hiking trails managed by the local Fontenelle Nature Association. The trails sparkled with spring azures that opened like tiny flashes of blue neon and closed to become brown flakes disappearing in the litter-thawed ground. A barred owl perched on a bare branch in a mottled brown coat that would have made him invisible except for Mark's keen eyes. As the owl watched us with the intensity of a staring contest, I wondered who would blink first. We did.

On to Grand Island, via the old Lincoln Highway, we rode through miles and miles of cornfields. The nation's first transcontinental highway, completed in 1913, running from Times Square in New York City to Lincoln Park in San Francisco, it marked the beginning of the modern U.S. roadway system. Just north of Lincoln, a turnoff led to the Jack Sinn State Memorial Wildlife Management Area. The management area protects an inland salt marsh, a rare wetland that is vanishing in part because of the very roads that allowed us access. In "A Salt Marsh Reclamation" from *Landscape with Figures: The Nonfiction of Place*, Lisa Knopp (2007) describes the plants and animals that inhabit these marshes. One of the rarest insects in North America, the salt creek tiger beetle, whose population may be as few as seven hundred, is found here and nowhere else. A short distance into the marsh, I noticed what looked like saltwort (*Salicornia rubra*) and a common salt grass (*Distichlis spicata var. stricata*), but still being winter, the plants were dry brown and difficult to identify. I didn't see anything that resembled the tiger beetle. Empty shotgun shells littered the ground around a sign that read "No Hunting," and crushed beer cans added an abrupt metallic splash of color to the dun landscape.

A grasshopper pinged onto my pant legs, but on close inspection, it turned out to be a black ground beetle. It made me think of the grasshopper known as the Rocky Mountain locust (*Melanoplus spretus*) once common in this region. In *Locust: The Devastating Rise and Mysterious Disappearance of the Insect That Shaped the American Frontier*, Jeffrey Lockwood (2004) tells the story of how this grasshopper "in vast ravenous armies of crop-eating swarms" devastated thousands of acres of crops. Some of the reports of besiegement were dreadful. One pioneer reported his family's clothes being "literally eaten from off their limbs." Such accounts turned the insect into "a plague of biblical proportion," and massive efforts to destroy the pest were enacted. By plowing up and cultivating the locusts' nursery grounds, they destroyed the insect's habitat. The eradication efforts proved so successful that the settlers managed not only to control the pest, but to eliminate the species completely. The species is now extinct. That we can exterminate one species (even one that destroys our food supply) and save another baffles me. I am always surprised at our reaction to what we perceive as threat. As a biologist who looks at the earth's species as our children, I see that there may be great differences among them and some can be quite destructive to us, but do we not love them all and wish for them to survive, even the most troublesome ones? (Well, maybe not mosquitoes.) Yet we don't seem able to grasp that the web of life is complex and with the loss of even one small irritating species, the ecology of an ecosystem may be changed. Yes, I know many consider the insect more than irritating, but why we cannot accommodate even a little loss for the sake of preserving a species, makes me wonder about our destructive egocentric ways.

While navigating the grid of Nebraska's back roads, Mark explained how rainfall regulated the original ecosystem of the high plains. The eastern part of the state with the heaviest rainfall was once tall grass prairies; the middle of the state was mixed prairie; and the west and most arid portion, was short grass prairie. Only about 1 percent of the original prairie is left and today the land is mostly cornfield, a crop that requires tremendous amounts of water. Because of the demand and the methods used to irrigate, the water table is dropping. Nearly every field we observed had a wheel of trusses connected with arched pipes that looked like a daisy chain of Eiffel Towers. The irrigation system called center-pivot irrigation throws water into the air but much of the water evaporates before it reaches the soil. Ian Frazier in *Great Plains* (1989) describes this system as "a span of irrigation pipe as much as a quarter mile long [that] makes a slow circuit like the hands of a clock." In an essay entitled "Affinity," Lisa Knopp writes about Frank Zybach, the native Nebraskan who invented center-pivot irrigation (Knopp 2007). Like all good biographers, Knopp strongly relates to and develops an affinity for him, describing him as an honest, ingenious man. Yet how often our best intentions and cleverest inventions that seem progressive, productive, and imaginative at the time can lead us down the path of squander. The irrigation method is not only wasteful and has reduced the water table, but has actually changed the humidity of the prairie lands.

The fields along the interstate near Grand Island were full of sandhill cranes. The crane corridor, as it is known, stretches from Lexington to Grand Island and is about eighty miles wide. The birds begin arriving from the southwest in March, feed along the river, and leave for their breeding grounds in northern Canada in April. That evening we stood with dozens of other crane watchers on a bridge overlooking the shallow Platte waiting for the birds to come in from the fields. In great loopy ribbons strung out over the horizon they began arriving and landing like falling leaves on the bare islands in the river.

The Platte River is so shallow and braided with mud flats it hardly seems right to call it a river. It could have been more of an arroyo, as James Michener (1974) in *Centennial* describes it, "the sorriest river in America…too thick to drink, too thin to plow." An account from 1836 by one of the local heroines from near my home, Narcissa Prentiss from Prattsburg, New York, chronicles the river as having putrid (stagnant) water and no trees. Loren Eiseley's (1957) description from *The Immense Journey*, however, is more poetic: "The Platte, a mile wide and an inch deep…where neither water nor land quite prevails…was the immense body of the continent itself, flowing…grain by grain, mountain by mountain, down to the sea." In an essay entitled "Braided," Liza Knopp (2002) tenderly recounts how she learned to braid her hair with a description of the Platte River, the river as ever intertwining, crisscrossed strands. All the many descriptions of this river that cuts the United States in half suggest there must be something about the Platte that inspires writing. Of course, I would be remiss if I didn't mention one of my least favorite quotes about the Platte River. Frederick Jackson Turner (the distinguished Harvard historian of the 1920s) is reported to have rebuked his daughter when she tried to contradict a visiting scholar with the comment, "Women's minds are like the Platte River—a mile wide and a foot deep" (Wickenden 2011: 73).

The following morning, wrapped in heavy coats, wool hats, and thick gloves, our group gathered at the Crane Meadows Nature Center for the fly out. Like a Pawnee war party, we trotted single file in the dark to a wooden blind along the river. The closer we got to the river, the louder the racket. Settling into the blind, no more than a tiny shed, we watched the birds through the cracks in the narrow plank slats. Just as the sky began to brighten, the volume turned up several notches. Then like mist rising from the surface of the river, the cranes began to lift up into the air. Drifting off in all directions and disappearing in the pale morning sky, the birds dissolved into the horizon. For an hour or more, the river fluttered with departure, and when the sun was fully up the river returned to quiet pools of shimmering water.

Out in the stubble fields the cranes spread out to feed, but they always kept a substantial distance from the road (and from us humans). We stopped on the roadside and Mark spent some time looking through the scope. "There it is," he whispered, "the whooping crane," and we watched the most rare bird in North America feeding among its smaller sandhill crane companions. I could not take my eyes off the bird, the way it stopped, cocked its head, almost posing, then elegantly strolled forward, stopping, and repeating its milk-glass pose. It was a ballet of white grace. Paul Johnsgard (1998) in *Crane Music: A Natural History of American Cranes* writes, "Cranes are the stuff of magic…" and I believe he is right.

South of Hastings in the region known as the Rainwater Basin, we traveled through cornfields so flat that we seemed to look up at the distant horizon. Miles of bunkers lined the highway like a fairway. These war middens, now mostly abandoned, seemed to reveal our country's warrior heart. Near an old brick munitions building, we pulled off the road and Mark pointed out a small prairie dog colony. Several black-tailed prairie dogs sat on the edges of their burrows like sentinels. When Mark whistled, imitating a red-tailed hawk, the little rodents reared upright, squealed, clapped their hands, and darted back into their holes. This hand-clapping behavior is part of their warning system, and I was reminded of my elementary teachers who used the clap method to get our attention.

Unfortunately, the prairie dog did not have an effective warning system against humans, for the species almost disappeared by the middle of the century. Paul Johnsgard's *Prairie Dog Empire: A Saga of the Shortgrass Prairie* (2005) and John L. Hoogland's *Conservation of the Black-tailed Prairie Dog: Saving North America's Western Grassland* (2005) recount how the population of prairie dogs declined nearly three orders of magnitude by the 1960s. Although conservation efforts have helped increase the numbers to around 2 percent of their original populations, with the near demise of this keystone species, one hundred and seventy other species that depended on prairie dogs for food and shelter also lost their habitat and food source. Populations of ferret and kit fox and species of western hawks significantly declined in tandem with the prairie dogs.

Against the endless cornfields, the munitions depot seemed to reflect our nation's history. In less than a hundred years, Americans had moved out onto the plains and converted the largest grassland in North America to cornfields. It made some people wealthy. In mid-century, America won the war and we became not only rich but powerful. Sometimes I wonder what we have done with our enormous wealth and power. Would the challenge of "to whom much is given, much is expected" be actualized, or would our wealth always be on the broken backs of extinct species?

The next morning we were out before dawn again, this time looking for prairie chickens. Driving the wet, gluey back roads to the Taylor Ranch was a slippery affair, and the fog was so dense, the fence along the road looked like solitary posts. The lek far out on the prairie was invisible as we stood and waited; an hour passed, then two, with only an occasional faint drumming. As if to make up for the lackluster performance of the prairie chickens, meadowlarks began to sing, and their flute-notes filled the morning. As one lark finished its lilting song, another began, then another and another until the prairie was filled with rounds of lark music.

From the foggy prairie, we headed north into sandhill country and arrived at the Calamus Reservoir, a large lake formed by the damming of the Calamus River. Even though the landscape changed from flat prairie to rolling hills, we never lost connection with the Platte in that watery web of Nebraska river tributaries, where the Calamus joins the North Loop, which joins the South Loop to become the loop that joins the Platte around Columbus.

The Calamus River gets its name from the sedge that grows along its shores. Calamus (*Acorus calamus*), also known as sweet flag, produces a fragrant oil, called asarone, that is mildly psychotropic. And there did seem something mystical about those waters. Above the lake a dozen white pelicans glided in circles around the day moon. Like flash cards, they turned white when the sun hit the tops of their wings and black when the light caught their black wingtips. In a grove of trees alongshore, a tree full of cedar waxwings was a choir of penny whistles, and the dense stick pattern of an eagle's nest in another tree added to the hypnotic atmosphere of the lake.

Turning off the main road we pulled into Calamus Outfitters where Bruce Switzer and his wife, Sue, greeted us like long lost friends. A couple in contrast, they could have been ring-necked pheasants; he, a large vibrant fellow; she, a round soft-colored woman. Standing over six feet tall, with a red kerchief around his neck, in his rugged ten-gallon Stetson, faded jeans and cowboy boots, he was the perfect image of a rancher, and his blue eyes sparkled when he talked about his ranch. He and his son were moving slowly into the ecotourism business, because cattle ranching is such an up and down proposition; some years it's good, some, bad. Their outfitters business and the small cabins for vacationers would take up the slack in the lean years. Bruce updated us on the status of the eagle's nest, telling us how the mother eagle was still sitting on the eggs, and any day now he expected mouths to appear, needing to be fed. He reminded me of Dayton Hyde, a rancher who wrote the children's story *Sandy: The True Story of a Rare Sandhill Crane That Joined Our Family* (1968). Some of these tough old rawhide cowboys have such tender hearts for the animals of their world.

On the way back to Omaha, we stopped at the grave of Susan O'Haile, who was thirty-four when she died of cholera. As a microbiologist, I know how easily cholera can be avoided: if only she had known the bacterium was waterborne and that by boiling water for ten minutes, the organisms could have been killed, and she might not have been just another pioneer statistic on the road to the colonization of the west. Although her husband moved on, he returned ten years later to erect a small stone where she was buried. Above the ruts of the wagon wheels that engraved the Oregon Trail onto the prairie, we stood on the small hill and looked out over the open plains. With the grasses rolling like ocean swells, I wondered if Susan O'Haile was a woman who had been, in the words of the native Nebraskan Tillie Olsen in *Tell Me a Riddle* (1961), "forced to move to the rhythms of others." Did she feel compelled to follow her husband to the new land, a land full of dangers and isolation, or did she relish the chance to move to a new place with hopes of a better future, only to be struck down by a bacterium carried in birds feces, dropped, and then drifted on the plankton in the stagnant waters of the Platte?

Our last stop for gas at a busy truck stop was a quick one. Ahead of me in line at the checkout counter, an elderly woman looked distraught. Her eyes were red, her nose was runny, and she was pale. She said, "I'm exhausted, been driving ten hours. Me and my husband run into a terrible snowstorm outside Denver. The roads was so slick and iced, we barely crawled. Accidents all over the highway; was a miracle we got through. We got another sixteen hours to make it to Minnesota." She was trying to get home for a funeral.

We are a restless nation, always moving, looking for new places, new sights, new insights, or simply returning home. Like the cranes, we seem to be constantly on the move, even if it is on a predetermined route. But unlike the cranes we may have become alienated from the land and each other, and this restlessness may be a yearning to return to a sense of belonging. Seeking place can evoke such desperation. That desperation may find resolution in those who are leaving a legacy, not one of conquering the west or the world, not one of accumulating wealth and power, but one of making good places in both words and actions. The preserves, the sanctuaries, and the refuges along the Platte represent signs that many Americans are trying through sound conservation and restoration ecology to leave a better future, a better place. And those crafted writers of the plains who lovingly wrote in the past about their place in America's heartland and the writers who write today may be doing that as well.

CHAPTER 3.

Along the Chattahoochee: United States, Alabama, Eufaula National Wildlife Refuge

The woman at the Southern Accents gift shop wanted to sell me something, but I was having no part of it. For one thing, she reminded me of my Aunt Pearl, whose syrupy southern charm drove me nuts. My aunt was always trying to look like Rosalyn Carter or Lady Bird Johnson with her coiffured hair and dress suits. I suspected the shop lady, like my aunt, was a fan of Andy Griffith and perhaps sold real estate on the side. "Well, honey," she said, 'I can't seem to get you to buy a thing, can I?" her words dripping with sugary disapproval. It took some self-control not to say, "No'm," and drawl it out for four or five minutes, but I politely said in the most proper accent-free English that I was just browsing.

The gift shop was on the way to the refuge and my companion birders wanted to stop. I, on the other hand, wanted to leave the moment we entered the shop, having never been much of a honeysuckle incense, watermelon-colored placemats, matching kitchenware sort of person. As we drove through Eufaula to the refuge, the old antebellum homes with their moss-draped stately live oaks and ancient magnolias drifted by. I half expected to see the iconic Hattie McDaniel emerge from the doorway and wave us a big welcome. Old plantation homes don't have much appeal for me either, but Eufaula's long history of southern-hood has created a popular tourist attraction for those interested in reliving the Old South. In the 1800s, cotton and timber were shipped up the Chattahoochee River, making the town a thriving port city for steamboats. The old homes in this former major shipping and trading center reflected the accumulated wealth of those enterprises. Today the largest business second to WalMart is Alatech Health Care, the biggest state-of-the-art condom production facility in the United States. I don't think I will even comment on that evolution.

The wildlife refuge was established in 1963, after the damming of the Chattahoochee River by the U.S. Army Corps of Engineers. The reservoir formed was named the Walter F. George Reservoir, but the locals call it Lake Eufaula. The refuge along the reservoir is within the Mississippi flyway so it is an excellent place for birding. A seven-mile loop road allows access to several rookeries and extensive mud flats. With our binoculars ready, we rode slowly along the graveled road, scanning the wax myrtle thickets and the phragmites. The yellow flashes of prothonotary and yellow-rumped warblers gave the roadside a smiley-face look, while a rookery on the opposite side of the impoundment sprouted feather-trees with blue and white ornaments—snowy, great, and little egrets, great blue and little blue herons. Wood storks standing in the shallows were as still as old tree snags, and anhingas on fallen logs aired their wings in a daisy chain of black thunderbirds. Off in the distance, a flock of glossy ibis dipping and straining the mud turned the waters maroon with their reflections.

The trail that circled the impoundment was on a narrow grassy levee. We strolled along with our binoculars moving from one tree to the next trying to identify migratory warblers. Around a sharp bend, we were on the alligator before we knew it. She was sprawled out in the middle of the path still as stone, her eyes closed. When we halted abruptly, she opened one ghastly eye and looked at us with a terrifying reptilian gaze. No sweet pretense about the loveliness of nature in that eye. No clever, whimsical narrative such as that in Karen Russell's mythical *Swamplandia* (2011) where the heroine's mother is the star attraction as a champion alligator wrestler. The message conveyed in that eye was clearly designed to evoke terror, the terror of labeling us as prey. Hypnotic, almost paralyzing, it took me back to the time when we were cowering little mammals. It said, "You are helpless and I will eat you." Barry Lopez refers to this predator and prey interaction as "the conversation of death" (Lopez 1978: 94) and in that moment, I understood why. We backed up rapidly and as quietly as we could, aware of the danger and immediacy of needing to move in the direction of away.

There are many stories of alligator encounters, ranging from urban legends of sewer gators in New York City to pet killings in subdivisions built near wetlands, but a lighthearted one I recall from some years ago around a Christmas bonfire on the Mississippi River levee was a variation of one told by the mystery writer Margaret Maron in *Killer Market* (1997). Two good ol' boys were driving home late one night after an evening at the local watering hole. After hours of beer guzzling and pool, the driver swerved to avoid hitting a nutria, and the pickup ended up in a deep ditch on the roadside. They got out to look over the damage. In the headlights, an alligator swam toward them. It grabbed for one of the fellow's legs and tried to pull him under. The other fellow jumped on the gator's back and wrestled it, jabbing and stabbing with his knife until it was finally still. They threw it in the back of the pickup and headed home. The next morning they went to check on the carcass and found an old tire tread, wrapped around itself, full of knife punctures.

This humorous story is a tall tale but in reality alligator encounters are no joking matter; their attacks can be gruesome. In 2006 Annmarie Campbell, who had gone snorkeling in a creek in Florida's Ocala National Forest, was grabbed by an alligator and her lungs crushed (Lemonick 2006). Two other women were attacked in a nearby waterway and killed that same year. The Florida Fish and Wildlife Conservation Commission records about seven human attacks every year. From 1948 to 2004, three hundred and thirty four attacks and fourteen fatalities were recorded in Florida while overall statistics for the United States totaled three hundred and seventy six attacks, with twenty three fatalities (Langely 2005). Like any large wild predator, alligators can be a real danger if humans get too close.

The alligator is an ancient predator, and fossil records indicate it was gobbling down small and not-so-small prey two hundred and thirty million years ago, long before we humans were around. In the crocodile family, it is the largest reptile in North America and lives an average of fifty years. Its reptilian nature seems somewhat contradictory considering the maternal behavior of the female when raising its young. A mother alligator will stay near her nest protecting her young until they hatch, and when they begin to peep, she will tenderly carry them from the nest to the water in her mouth.

In the 1960s the species was close to extinction due to massive killings to make shoes and purses. I remember my Aunt Pearl had an alligator purse that she carried on special occasions and bragged about how expensive it was; it was from Neiman Marcus, she said. With a large brassy clasp, it was the color of root beer with small bubbles that got bigger toward the bottom. I never made the connection that it was the skin of an endangered animal. Today, alligator populations are now estimated at well over several million, and while placed on the endangered species list in 1967, it was removed in 1987; it still remains on the threatened species list.

Leaving the refuge we noticed that evening had come and puffed up the horizon with carnelian clouds against a cerulean sky. Despite the faux down-home, living-is-easy, old-southern-charm pretense of the town and the area that surrounds the refuge, the refuge itself is a genuine place. It is land set aside not for the exploitation of wildlife, or land where fellow humans' labor is exploited; it is not based on the exploitation of the river or the natural resources, but a place set aside to protect wildlife and to offer refuge for many species of the coastal south. It may have been created by damming up the river, but I like to think it has transcended that environmentally unsound practice to become a place of safety for some animals. While some hunting is allowed, it is not a hunting ground for massive duck kills. Its mission is the protection of habitats for migratory birds, water-fowl, raptors, and marsh birds, and it protects threatened species such as the American alligator. It is a wildlife sanctuary in a genuine sense.

CHAPTER 4.

From the Himalayas the Brahmaputra Flows: India, Assam and Arunachal Pradesh

Ten years after my first visit to India, I had hoped a repeat visit might resolve the problem of why my experience of India did not correspond to what others report. The popular literature is full of wondrous descriptions of India as a visitor's paradise. With all the attributes of a thoughtful traveler's quests, India is one of the world's oldest civilizations; it is multicultural, multilingual, multiracial; it is the largest democracy in the world, the birthplace of several religions (Buddhism, Hinduism, Sikhism, and Jainism) and the country that has given the modern world the philosophy of nonviolence; and as an agricultural and rural land, two-thirds of its population lives in villages. All these qualities are ones I admire, so the paradox of my experience and what is written about the country left me puzzled.

My second trip did not resolve the conflict. In fact, I found my experience of India even more disheartening than ever. The tour began with a visit to the Okhla Bird Sanctuary near Delhi. A small one and four-tenths square-mile refuge along the Yamuna River, Okhla Bird Sanctuary is one of India's 466 Important Bird Areas (IBAs). Its grasslands, thorny scrublands, and wetlands webbed with trails bordering the river were in sharp contrast to the city's high-rises that rose like an endless ragged edge across the lake, a lake created by the damming of the river. The trails through the reed beds (mostly *Typha angusatata* and *Phragmites maxima*) were flooded, but we managed to walk most of them, spotting painted storks, prinias, chiffchaffs, and many duck species. The sanctuary claims to provide habitat to over four hundred species of birds, and for our group, it provided a quiet afternoon in contrast to the congested city of Delhi.

The flight out of Delhi for Guwahati, the capital of Assam in northeast India, left early the next morning. The plan was to travel by jeep, first to Nameri National Park, continue north into the Himalayans to Arunachal Pradesh and Eaglenest Wildlife Sanctuary, backtrack down into the lowlands to Kaziranga National Park, and finally head back to Guwahati, Delhi and then home.

Nameri National Park, situated in the foothills of the eastern Himalayas, was originally part of a larger forest reserve; only since 1998 has it been established as a national park. We arrived at Eco Camp and settled in for a three-day stay. The camp consisted of a single open-air dining tent filled with wooden picnic tables, and a circle of canvas tents mounted on concrete platforms, each containing cots and a permanent bathroom with toilet and shower. Our bathroom was decorated with wildlife, lines of marching ants along the concrete floor, brown snails sliding over the porcelain sink and several leeches in the shower stall. Once we removed the creatures to the outdoors, I tried the cot and to my surprise, it collapsed like a lead weight. After the staff fixed the cot with much ado, and we had an evening meal of rice and a too-spicy curry stew, I settled in for the evening. It had been a long day of travel—the flight from Delhi to Guwahati and then the drive to the park—but a good night's rest was not on the agenda. Around midnight a storm rolled in—the wind picked up, and the rains began. The rain beat so fiercely against the tents it woke the entire camp, and with the gale-like winds, the tents bulged and flapped, filling the night with a loud popping and roaring. The noise went on for hours, until around 2 a.m., when I heard a loud whoosh and crash. Someone yelled a warning, and when I looked out several flashlights were moving around the pitch-black camp. Electricity was out. Another voice rang out, "it's all right, just a small tree down." When the heavy rain and wind finally calmed, I was able to go back to sleep. The next morning when I opened my tent flap and peeked out, an enormous palm tree was lying right next to my tent. It had missed my tent by inches.

I soon forgot the near collision of the palm tree and my tent as the morning unfolded. Jan Hansen, our guide, had hired a local crew to take us rafting, and the morning was a dreamy float down the white rock Jia Bhoroli River. The source of the river is the snowmelt of the Himalayas so the waters were crystal clear. There was enough white water to make it fun, but not so much as to make it dangerous, and with sunlight sparkling off the cold mountain waters and the outline of the peaks of the Himalayas in the background, the scenery was stunning. The crackling water running over pebbles was the only sound that filled the quiet. Seeing half a dozen rare ibis bills feeding along the river added to the mornings delight.

In the early afternoon most of the group left for a birding trek into the park's grasslands while I stayed in camp and talked with Jeb Das, the camp manager. He explained that Eco Camp was a part of Nameri National Park System, a system that included a number of protected areas. The park's largest problem was habitat destruction from illegal timber harvesting, especially the valuable hardwood known as amari (*Amoora wallichii*), but reforestation efforts such as planting saplings were ongoing. Because this is a sub-Himalayan forest, a habitat that has almost disappeared due to lumbering and cropland conversion, the preserve is trying to restore this ancient forest type. Jeb also talked about the pigmy hog breeding and release program. Thirteen pigmy pigs were currently held in captivity and plans to breed and release them were under way. Programs to help local women start small businesses by selling their crafts at the camp's gift shop and a number of community events to get the locals involved in the park's mission were also in progress. Finally, Jeb mentioned several research projects on butterflies and moths. His enthusiasm for the park and its projects made it obvious why conservation efforts were going so well.

The remaining afternoon, I watched a flame-back woodpecker working the tree outside my tent (one I was glad to see standing) while the camp staff played cricket on the commons. The joy these young men seemed to be taking in this British sport was fun to watch and added to the congenial atmosphere of the well-run camp.

The second day passed with birding treks to several remote parts of the park, and the following day we were off to Eaglenest Wildlife Sanctuary. The drive into the foothills of the Himalayans along a steep narrow winding road took us through several military checkpoints and the army town of Tenga. The strong military presence along the Chinese border was the result of recent tensions between the two countries. It would take all day on that harrowing road to reach the sanctuary.

Eaglenest Wildlife Sanctuary ranges in elevation from 1,640 to 10,663 feet, is the largest contiguous closed-canopy forest tract in Arunachal Pradesh, and is part of the Kameng Protected Area Complex (KPAC). KPAC encompasses around one thousand three hundred and fifty square miles and includes four wildlife sanctuaries, Nameri National Park, several forest preserves, a tiger reserve, and an elephant reserve. All camps in Eaglenest are temporary; they close during the rainy season (April and May) and it was March, just on the cusp of the rainy season. Our first two nights at Lama Camp took a bit of adjusting, as the accommodations were quite rustic. Tents mounted on bamboo platforms were positioned along the steep, hair-pinned road creating a two-tiered row. The fexible bamboo flooring bounced when we walked on it, making it feel like a trampoline. The beds consisted of sleeping bags thrown on top of the platforms. Communal toilets were flushable, and had to be manually filled with water from the mountain stream. The stream also provided wash water for a simple sink, with no showers. The water was very, very cold.

On the first evening, a local Sherpa introduced our group to the flora of the indigenous eastern broadleaf forests. Several species of oak (*Quercus* species) and Indian horse chestnut (*Aesculus indica*) were the most common species (Choudhury 2003). He claimed there were over fifty species of Rhododendron—some shrubby bushes, some tall trees. *R. arboretum* and *R. alta* were the most abundant and were currently in bloom. Species of magnolia were also abundant. He warned us to avoid a poisonous plant called elephant nettle (*Dendrocnide sinuata*). He ended his lecture by telling us that some of the older trees become so heavy with epiphytes (lichens and mosses) the branches break off and fall onto the road, sometimes hitting people.

The first night was not too uncomfortable, but on the second night a cold front moved in and the temperature dropped dramatically. The staff gave us hot water bottles to put in our sleeping bags, but the heat soon gave out and the bags had to be jettisoned. In the morning, I found myself tangled in many layers of my warmest clothing.

The one road in and out of the region was the site of all our birding activities. Walking the road looking for the various species of woodpeckers and treecreepers, Jan mentioned that this was the route the Dalai Lama took when he escaped from Tibet into India. Somehow what seemed a rather monotonous dirt road with drab shrubs and dwarfed trees took on a more interesting aspect when I thought about walking the same road as the Dalai Lama. Yet I wondered if that feeling of exhilaration might have had more to do with the sun shining, for it had warmed up considerably.

The following day we were off to Bompu camp. The road led to Tibet, Jan mentioned once again, and again the idea created a small thrill, but as the jeeps climbed up and over the pass at 7,000 feet, it became narrower and muddier, less exciting and more nerve-wracking. The view from the jeep windows was often a steep thousand-foot drop to the same road below. Because of the border issues with China, a jeep full of armed soldiers would occasionally zoom past us, throwing up mud and dust. At the pass we descended to around 6,000 feet as a thick mist rolled in and visibility declined.

Much to my dismay, Bompu Camp was even more primitive than Lama Camp. Two rows of thin tents and tarps that flapped in the constant wind had been mounted on cement slabs. Toilets were simple holes in the ground, and beds were hard, wooden platforms covered with thin mats. Some of the tents had only hammocks and not everyone in the group got a sleeping bag. The first night another storm rolled in, the wind howled, and a torrential rain fell all night long. The tents snapped and crackled all night, and I imagined them becoming airborne and me ending up in Oz, but dawn's light revealed all the tents in place and we didn't lose anyone.

I can't remember why we had to get up at 4:30 a.m. in order to be in the bamboo forest by 7 p.m.—maybe it was to see the rare sparrow, Bugun liocichla (*Liocichla bugumorum*), although no one did. Some of the group claimed to have seen it the day before near Lama Camp, but there was a lot of discussion and its sighting was ruled out. I tried to make the best of the day, but try as I might, I was unable to see any of the indigenous animals of the bamboo forest—no red pandas, no flying squirrels, no macaques—however, there were plenty of treecreepers, flowerpeckers, leafbirds, sunbirds, and many species of warblers. The vegetation at this lower elevation looked tropical, with bamboo, ferns, lianas, palms, and plants with frond-like leaves, but it certainly didn't feel tropical. The cold and damp penetrated my thermal underwear and thick pants and even my heavy fleece jacket seemed useless against the wind. I often found myself sitting in the jeep to avoid the bitter cold.

On the second night in Bompu Camp, my hot water bottle leaked (it was a flimsy red rubber thing) and my blanket and clothes got soaked, which made the cold even worse. So by the following morning, I was more than ready to leave. Back down the mountains, we stopped overnight once again at Lama Camp for another uncomfortable night in cold tents. This time I took more notice of the information posters mounted on the bamboo walls of the dining hut. One of them had a photograph of the bird-watcher and conservationist Ramona Athreya. The poster described how he had discovered a new species of bird, the Bugun liocichla in 2006, which was considered quite a significant event in India. He had also been instrumental in establishing Eaglenest as a bird sanctuary. In hindsight, I was a little disappointed for not trying to get a look at the bird, even if just a brief flicker of its rare feathers.

After Lama Camp we left the cold, wet Himalayas and descended to the lowlands and onto the Brahmaputra's floodplain. The bridge over the river, with the Karbi Anglong hills rising in the distance, was over a mile long, and below it many islands and flats braided the vast brown river. I remembered the news reports the previous year of the monsoons that had flooded the region, displacing over a quarter million people. The shallowness of the river and its geography made the floods understandable.

We arrived at Kaziranga National Park in late afternoon and made our way to a private lodge outside the park. On the way, a group of one-horned Indian rhinoceros feeding in a grassy area along the roadside provided a stopping point for a rare sight.

Kaziranga, a UNESCO World Heritage site, has two-thirds of the world's population of these rare rhinos (two thousand three hundred and twenty-nine of a world population of three thousand in 2012) as well as one of the highest densities of Bengal tigers in the world (one hundred and eighteen in 2006). The park is also considered a world "biodiversity hot spot" because of the abundance of rare species found there. Over four hundred and seventy species of birds have been reported and forty nine are globally threatened; of the thirty five species of mammals that make the park home, fifteen are threatened.

Access to Kaziranga National Park is by park jeeps or elephants and our group took advantage of both to explore the park. The first morning we made our way to the park's entrance early, hopped into the park jeeps, and headed into the park. The jeeps were even smaller than those we came in on, so everyone had to squeeze into an even smaller space, and they bounced so heavily that without holding on, a body might fly off into the road. A twenty five-mile long and eight-mile wide stretch of shoreline on the Brahmaputra, the park is mostly savannas and grasslands dotted with tropical broadleaf forests and webbed with channels. It has been called Asia's Serengeti and that morning a mist from the river gave the landscape a misty, gauzy look. But within the hour, the mist burned off and temperatures soared. The largest mammals were the elephants and they roamed everywhere. A small herd crossed one of the many channels, wading playfully through the waters and sloshing to the other side, where they moved onto the savanna and dissolved in the tall grass. The drive later that afternoon was even hotter, with temperatures rising into the 90s, and by evening I was wiped out from the heat and the bouncy jeeps.

The next morning the group, minus me, went on the elephant trek. I hated to miss the elephant ride and the tea plantation, but everything had caught up with me. The cold, the heat, the spicy food, and the rough riding rendered me unable to get out of bed.

I figured with a day's rest I might bounce (pardon the pun) back. As luck would have it, the day was full of excitement and the others returned with tales of riding elephants, descriptions of a tiger slinking in the grass, and the tea plantation as an almost mythical walk through lands as quiet and serene as a garden. The group learned how tea was processed, how only the young leaves were picked, and no one encountered a king cobra. But the tiger spotting was the highlight for everyone, and the primary topic of the evening dinner. With India's population of tigers representing three-quarters of the Asian population—only three thousand two hundred tigers are left in the wild—the sighting was quite rare. Leave it to me to miss the best day.

The drive back to Guwahati to catch our flight to Delhi included one final stop—the rubbish dump—to look for greater adjutants. Standing five feet tall like midget kings of the dump, these giant storks, called hargila, or "bone-swallowers" in Sanskrit, feed on carrion and offal. Their English name, greater adjutant, (a senior military officer's assistant), refers to the fact that they can remain motionless for hours. Legs stained and sooted with their own droppings, which are said to offer relief from the heat, they have massive wedged bills, skin heads, and bloated leather neck pouches the color of dried blood. Making for a bird worthy of ghoulish myths, legend has it they feed on partly burnt corpses floating down the Ganges, and folklore claims that a piece of their flesh, eaten along with betel, cures leprosy. Killed off in large numbers because they were believed to be unclean, they are now on the endangered species list.

The dump, with its miles of garbage and stench was an experience that would disturb me for a long time. The stench was so powerful I would not get out of the van, but the closed window framed the birds and the rag pickers as clearly as a Brueghel painting of medieval hell. A woman squatted in the water among the hyacinths washing clothes. She would occasionally splash water onto her face as if cleaning herself while her children played in the dirt yard. It was one of the most disturbing and poignant sights I witnessed during my tour of India.

While the flight back to Delhi was uneventful, the overlay in the city to make the necessary connections home was depressing. I was pestered and harassed by men on the streets every time I walked from the hotel to a nearby kiosk, and the soot and grime of the streets was dismal. It did not help matters to recall the more numerous reports that seem to be coming out of India regarding the brutal rape of women. The piles and piles of trash and garbage evoked such a feeling of disorder and uncleanness. The skeletal bodies of the bike-taxi drivers as they slept in the streets on dingy pads, the miserable rib-showing cows that roamed everywhere, and the multitudes that lived in cardboard boxes, were only a few of the many sights that made me sad.

After returning from India, I wrote the following poem as part of my attempt to resolve the disparity of my experience of India with what others report:

From the Himalayas the Brahmaputra Flows

At Lama Camp the red rhododendrons bloomed
white magnolias mimicked the snow peaks of Gori Chen
a fairy-fantail flicked its tail playful as a folding fan
below a full moon illuminating tattered prayer flags.

At Kaziranga a young woman sari-wrapped
in hibiscus red washing clothes along a muddy stream
lifted her smile and waved as we rode by.
Such scant small beauties.

Is this all I get for a month of motion sickness
food I cannot eat, diarrhea and nausea, grime
and dirt, the damp, the cold, the heat, the lack

of sleep, the money spent?

Our American guide gave his scope to our Indian guide
loaned his space blanket to another for warmth.
A young man pedaled his ice cream cart
through miles of garbage in the Guwahati dump.

Then the fellow at the airport who caught me
when I nearly fainted from the heat and wheel-chaired
me through the boarding lines- such small acts of kindness.
I had asked for more. I had asked for many

Great beauties, to witness scores of kindness
but there were few. Times I had to pull
all my survival tactics to get through
the bitter nights.

And still I asked for more
knowing this is the place where the Buddha sat
beneath the ficus tree and understood
this is all we get.

I have found India a reality that still remains unresolvable. It may be the proverbial concept of "east meets west but never the two shall twine;" it may be the vast indifference to the poverty and grime I observed; it may be the feeling of insignificance evoked by the presence of so many people and the conclusion that I am only one of billions who occupy this beautiful earth; it may be the fact that compassion is hard to acquire when one is physically uncomfortable and borderline unwell. But regardless of my personal perceptions of India, conservation efforts in this country are laudable. And that is hopeful. It is inspiring to know that in a place so alien, so depressingly poor, there are those who care deeply for the natural world and are providing sanctuary for the earth's creatures.

COASTAL LANDS

CHAPTER 5.

The Durango Highway, San Blas, and Marismas Nacionales: Mexico, West Coast

A year after visiting the Baja, the plan was to return to Mexico's west coast, starting in Mazatlán, traveling the Durango Highway inland through the Sierra Madres, and then swinging south to San Blas. A hundred years ago, Mazatlán, San Blas, and most of these coastal Mexican towns were tropical pestholes where outbreaks of typhoid, cholera, and malaria occurred and visitors did not go. Today Mazatlán is a Mexican Riviera resort town with high-rises and condos strung out along a tan beach lined with palm trees, eateries, and shops. Warm sea breezes blow, brown pelicans drift across the sky, and high waves attract surfers and beach walkers. The rendezvous point to meet our guide, Jan Hansen (Otus Asio tours 2011) and our birding group was the Hotel La Siesta. A plaque near the entrance of the hotel had a quote from Jack Kerouac's (1957) *On the Road.* It read "the only people for me are the mad ones, the ones who are mad to live, mad to talk, mad to be saved, desirous of everything at the same time, the ones that never yawn or say a common place thing but burn, burn." In the lobby of the old hotel, three ancient trees, strangler figs with big boat-like leaves and long hanging aerial roots, lent an exotic air to the place. Jack Kerouac and strangler figs seemed a promising way to start a trip.

A stroll about town took me to an old gothic church where I stopped to light a candle for a friend battling cancer. The huge gray stone church, the Basilica of the Immaculate Conception, looked more like a fortress than a house of worship but maybe that was the point. One oddity stood out; above each stain-glassed window was the Star of David. The story went like this: when the church was being constructed in the mid-1800s, they ran out of money before it was completed. The builders went to the wealthiest folks in the community and asked for their help. They were Jewish and they agreed to donate the money if a Star of David would be placed above each window. When I went to light a candle, I noticed the candles were electric. The way it worked was to make a donation, flip a switch, and an electric flame would flicker. I had to smile at the practicality of a church that would agree to another religion's icons and that allowed its prayers to rise on the wings of electric modernity.

The Durango Highway, Federal Highway 40 or the inter-oceanic highway, runs east-west from the Gulf Coast of Mexico through the central Mexican Plateau to the Pacific Coast. From Durango to Mazatlán, it crosses the Sierra Madre Occidental range and becomes the Espinoza del Diablo, the Devil's Backbone; or the Road of Three Thousand Curves. It is well known as an impor-tant birding route because it runs through diverse habitats, and birders come from all over the world to see the numerous endemic species of the region.

Scraggly acacia and thorn shrub gave way to oaks and manzanita as we drove up into the foothills of the Sierra Madres to the vil-lage of Copala, our home base for several nights. The village was a far cry from the resort coast of Mazatlán. Roosters crowed at all hours of the day and night, donkeys brayed, dogs barked, and the grinding of old truck transmissions made for a noisy stay, but the banana coconut cream pie at the small restaurant next to the hotel partly made up for the commotion.

Our group was up the first morning before daybreak for the drive into the Sierra Madres along the Durango Highway. We soon discovered the highway lived up to its name, Road of Three Thousand Curves. Its winding narrow switchbacks were treacherous in the dark morning hours before sunup, and every time a large cargo truck came barreling down around one of the hairpin turns, I felt my heart leap into my throat, my stomach churn, and my fingers turn white from clutching the door handles. We climbed from 1,200 to 6,800 feet, where the forest became the typical pine-oak of the Sierra Madre Occidentals, a forest composed of over twenty-seven species of pine and nearly that many species of oak. We pulled off into a clearing, parked, and walked the trail along the canyon known as Barranca del Liebre, or "gorge of the hares." We saw no hares, but a dozen or more tufted jays were flying about. Huge noisy birds with blue-black backs, black bibs, and white Mohawk head-crowns, they were hanging out in the treetops. As the sun rose, the ridges and canyons turned golden. The pines, the oaks, and even a wire fence gleamed with the gilded hue of early morning. The higher we walked, the more intense the light became. It felt like we were walking into the heavens.

In 2005, the land around the canyons became a conservation easement known as the Tufted Jay Preserve. Three groups, Ejido El Palmito, a logging cooperative of sixty-four local families who owned the land communally; Pronatura Noroeste, the regional chapter of Mexico's oldest and most prestigious conservation organization; and CONABIO, the National Commission for the Use and Knowledge of Biodiversity, negotiated to create a protected area (Miller 2009). Tufted jays were being heavily impacted by logging and their populations were declining, so the conservation groups agreed to pay the collective (the families who owned it) to cease logging the nine hundred and ninety acres that encompassed the San Diego and Rancho Liebre canyons. The agreement extends for a period of thirty years, so the tufted jays will have a protected home until a more permanent arrangement can be made. Many conservations groups are continuing to work to make this preserve a permanent sanctuary.

The preserve provided not only jays, but a number of other birds—a red-faced warbler, a red warbler, and a hermit thrush. I imagined this lovely thrush returning to New York (like me) in a few months and filling the northeastern woods once again with its lilting song, the song I think of as essential spring.

On our way from Copala to the coastal town of San Blas, a shade-grown coffee and mango plantation near the village of Tecuitata offered a walk through hills covered in coffee trees. This communal plantation is known for its sustainable farm practices. Although there is no clear legal definition of sustainable farming, it is generally accepted and recognized as "coffee grown in a manner that is kind to the environment and its people." As we watched the slow work of the coffee pickers and the intense labor required, it was a reminder of the effort expended for our morning brew. We then headed to San Blas for a few days stay at a local family-owned hotel and restaurant known as the Graza Canela.

Longfellow begins his poem "The Bells of San Blas" with the question, "What say the bells of San Blas?" and the first morning, waking to soft ringing and sunlight streaming in through the cracks in the curtains, I wondered if the answer was the comfort and serenity of home. The Hotel Garza definitely had a homey feel, with its colonial hacienda architecture, deep red tiles accented with bright blues and yellows, archways and stucco walls, but more than that, it was the Vasquez sisters who owned and managed the hotel that gave it the air of familiarity and hominess. One of the sisters or a family member was always running the desk or the restaurant, organizing the cleaning staff, or working in the gardens. Longfellow ends his poem with the line, "It is daybreak everywhere" and so as the first day in San Blas began with the ringing of bells and the soft rays of sunlight ushering in the day, the transcendental reassurance indeed felt like it was daybreak everywhere.

The early morning drive to the San Juan State Biosphere was another climb into mountainous terrain, but unlike the paved surface of the Durango Highway, the road was dirt and full of potholes. The ride was dusty and winding, and we bounced around for over an hour before arriving at the gates of the reserve. Our goal was to see the pale-billed woodpecker, a bird once abundant in the pine-oak forests of the Sierra Madres but whose populations, like the extinct imperial woodpecker (Mexico's ivory billed woodpecker), have been heavily impacted by habitat destruction, primarily logging.

Tim Gallagher in *Imperial Dreams* (Gallagher 2013) tells the story of his search for the imperial woodpecker in these mountains. The dangers he encounters from the rough terrain and Mexico's increasing violence and drug traffickers make for a frightening tale. In his search for the majestic imperial woodpecker, known as the pitoreal, he recounts some of the history of the Sierra Madre, its violent past and the devastation humans have wreaked on these mountain habitats. He collects evidence and proposes that not only did logging destroy the imperial woodpecker's habitat by removing all the old trees, logging interests paid to have the birds shot and poisoned so that populations plummeted. He reports that the forests are still being decimated today by both logging and the drug cartels, which clear-cut the forests to open fields for opium growing.

We walked the road for some time, and near a tiny roadside shrine, a pale-billed woodpecker perched in the upper branches of a pine. It was a male with a brilliant red head, crimson top notch, and a black back with white markings that nearly met in a distinct "V." To see this enormous rare woodpecker in its pine-oak forest home was clearly the highlight of the day.

The last day in San Blas was devoted to exploring the mangrove swamps with a morning boat trip through the marshes of La Tovara National Park and an evening ride to the La Tovara springs. We met Chencko, our guide, at the docks at 6 a.m., crawled into his flat-bottomed boat, and pushed off into the creamed-coffee waters of the San Cristóbal River. Mist rose from the water in long streamers as the sun warmed the river and, as it dissipated, the banks became visible, thick with mangroves. Not just one species, but all four species common to the American coasts were there: red mangroves (*Rhizophora mangles*), black mangroves (*Avicennia germinans*), white mangroves (*Laguncularia racemosa*), and button mangroves (*Conocarpus erectus*). Water birds were everywhere: bare-throated tiger herons, green herons, little blues, great blues, night herons, boat-billed herons, a mangrove cuckoo, and egrets. An army of caiman also dozed on the banks like lazy-eyed bandits among the gnarly mangroves.

Our guide maneuvered the boat off the main channel into a narrower canal and began poling it slowly through the catacombs of mangrove. The wicker roots of the mangroves hung down into the water like wishbones. Their brown ropy tangles, encrusted with salt and dried mud, had the look of prison bars and entrapment, and that's what mangroves do: they entrap sediment and keep the shoreline intact. Bromeliads were hairy stars, and epiphytic orchids clung to the branches, casting intricate shadows and exotic reflections onto the canals. The tunnels narrowed until the subtle yellow flowers of the red mangroves and their tough leathery leaves scraped the sides of the boat. I wondered if we would have to back out. But just as the tunnel seemed to close in on us completely, it opened a bit, became wider and wider until we were finally back on a main artery.

These marshes known as Marismas Nacionale represent the largest mangrove ecosystem (seven hundred and seventy square miles) on Mexico's west coast and are a RAMSAR site (WWW 2014). Some of the marshland is protected nationally (Flora and

Fauna Protection) and internationally as a Biosphere Reserve. While mangroves make up less than half of one percent of the world's forest, they store up to four times as much carbon as other tropical forests, so their role in the earth's carbon cycle is crucial. Since 1980, 20 percent of the world's mangrove forests have been lost, and one of the primary culprits is shrimp aquaculture (Warne 2011). Because shrimp farming is often the most viable means of economic growth for many coastal communities, it is difficult to pass laws that protect mangroves and restrict the development of shrimp farming. But a bigger threat is resort building. Mexico's tourist company (FONATUR) is designing a huge development in the area with plans to construct thousands of hotels, golf courses, marinas, and commercial centers (AIDA 2011). So what will happen to these mangrove swamps is anybody's guess. Given the way we view economic progress, the likelihood of losing these marshes seems imminent.

Later in the afternoon we were back on the river for a second ride, this time to the springs. The river was hot and still as we puttered further and further upstream. At the springs we stepped out of the boat and meandered about on a wooden deck. The water was crystal clear and inviting, so when our guide said we could swim, I was tempted. But then I remembered all the caiman we had seen strung out along the shore and thought better of it. Only later did I learn that recently a tourist had been attacked by a caiman, and that a croc had eaten a small dog belonging to another tourist.

As the sun slid lower, touching and then sinking below the horizon, the palms turned black and silhouetted against the crimson sky. Then the nighthawks came out! They buzzed about the river catching insects on the fly. One came so close that the woman sitting in the front of the boat ducked, but of course, these aerial masters would never collide with anything. Their echolocation system is as fine-tuned as those of bats. When the sky finally lost all its color and the last rays of sun faded, the fishing bats appeared and they in turn began zooming about the darkling sky. Also using echolocation, these large five-inch predatory bats detect the tiniest fish ripples and can catch up to thirty fish in an evening. We watched with fascination as a couple of them proved successful fishers.

Along the banks, pootoos nestled in old snags, looking like the primitive creatures they are. Related to the nightjars, these insect-eating birds were so well camouflaged in their perch, they could only be seen only because the guide knew exactly where to look (and they return to the same branch to roost). Their eyes reflected the headlights as two bright red spots in the crotch of an old dead tree among a ball of speckled feathers. As we made our way back to the marina, thousands of red caiman eyes burning bright (as "in the forest of the night") followed us, but as we drew nearer the docks, they became less ominous and more like the light of tiny tailgates.

The morning before leaving San Blas, I again lit a candle in the small chapel for my friend battling cancer. Above the altar, Howard Thurman's poem "Candles" (Alliance of Hope 2011) hung on the wall framed in gold. It read:

I will light candles this evening,

Candles of joy despite all sadness

Candles of hope where despair keeps watch

Candles of courage for fears ever present

Candles of peace for tempest-tossed days

Candles of grace to ease heavy burdens

Candles of love to inspire all my living

Candles that will burn all the year long.

The ride from San Blas back to Mazatlán to catch our flight home was a time for reflection. The corn and bean fields of the rich coastal plain zoomed by as I thought how intensely the Mexican Riviera had developed in such a short time. Mexico's west coast had become like so many of the world's coasts, the sea edge turned into resorts. The mountain habitats of the Sierra Madres were also suffering from destruction from logging and drug trafficking. Yet the efforts of local citizens, conservation groups at all levels, NGOs, governmental, state, national, and international organizations, are protecting as many of these habitats as they can.

I don't know if Jack Kerouac or Howard Thurman had ever considered conservationists as those whose lights shine or those who burn, but I think the folks who have been involved in preserving and protecting Mexico's west coast and the forests of the Sierra Madres are shining and burning in the most luminous ways. By continuing to protect these lands and keeping these important habitats from logging and development, they are candles that might burn not only all year but in continuum and perhaps in perpetuity.

CHAPTER 6.

Tropical Paradise: Ecuador, The Galapagos

The big diesel bus sped across Santa Cruz Island, ascending into the highlands where a blanket of fog known as "garua" muted the trees and shrubs. At the announcement of Twin Craters, everyone—all forty Japanese tourists, my traveling companion, and I—climbed out of the bus and milled around until we were told the trail was too dangerous to walk in the dense fog. Twin Craters, or Los Gemelos, is not actually a crater but rather a sink-hole formed by the collapse of the ground surface into a fissure where lava once flowed. Although we couldn't see the spectacular view, it was pleasant enough to be in the cloud forest and observe the evergreens, *Scalesia*. These giant daisy trees (standing about twenty feet tall) shrouded in mist were sprinkled with small white blossoms and covered with epiphytes of mosses, ferns, and bromeliads. Members of the sunflower family, the thirteen species of *Scalesia* endemic to the Galapagos are, like so many native species on the islands, threatened because of the impact of imported goats, pigs, and donkeys. Only remnant patches of this forest type exist now, but with efforts to restore the original forests, progress is being made to re-wild the island.

As we continued on to Puerto Ayora, the vegetation reflected the zonation of a typical volcanic island. The edge of the island is coastal mangroves (black, white, red, and button mangroves) and salt-tolerant plants; moving inward and upward to about two hundred feet, the arid lowlands have cactus (prickly pear cactus in the genus *Opuntia*), palo santo trees (*Bursera graveolens*), and acacia (*Acacia* species); the humid transition zones of the highlands support *Scalesia* (*S. pendunculata*) forests and the shrub forests of *Miconia* species; and at the very highest elevation, close to 3,000 feet and most humid, the pampas zone has only sedges and grasses.

In Puerto Ayora, the largest town on the island, the streets were lined with hotels and cafes, and tourists meandered along the sidewalks. We were dropped off at Finch Bay dock, where water taxis motored us across the bay to the Finch Bay Eco Hotel. As our Japanese travelers began crowding to get onto the boats, I had that irritable sensation one gets in large pushy crowds, that almost phobia-like feeling that there were too many of us. I wondered if the island had that same feeling. The number of tourists who visited the Galapagos in 2010 was 173,296 and for the past decade the average number of visitors has been around 150,000. For a place whose land mass is a little smaller than Yellowstone National Park, that seemed a lot of people, certainly not as many as the 3 million who go to Yellowstone every year, but still a lot.

The clatter of rolling luggage on the wooden walkway slats drowned out the twittering of finches as we made our way through the mangroves to the hotel. I reminded myself that I needed to view this place not as a tourist attraction, but as the Bethlehem of biology, the place where it all began. I admonished myself for not using another means of seeing it. As a biologist, I thought I should visit this archipelago, but I had chosen the most expedient way to do so. Without much research or planning, I had signed up for a four-day package from Quito with a commercial tour company, two days of which involved travel to and from. In hindsight it was not the most environmentally correct means of doing it, but convenience and expedience are appealing qualities and like most everyone, I sometimes fall victim to their allure. With places like Vietnam and Iraq hosting tourists, I should not have been surprised that the Galapagos ranked as such a popular tourist destination, but I did not expect quite so many people.

The Galapagos Archipelago consists of twelve main islands and twelve smaller ones, plus over a hundred rock islets. Established as an Ecuadorian National Park and Marine Reserve in 1959, the archipelago was recognized by UNESCO as a World Heritage Site in 1978 and declared a Biosphere Reserve in 1985. The reserve is funded by the Ecuadorian government, and the Charles Darwin Research Center. UNESCO in 2007 placed the islands on the danger list but withdrew it in 2010 when programs to protect its diversity were set into place. Such efforts, including the Isabela Project funded by several international groups, removed goats, pigs, and donkeys from three islands, Isabela, Santiago, and Pinta. At a cost of over $13 million, this might seem a rather expensive endeavor until one thinks of the cost of homes in certain upscale U.S. neighborhoods. The project was one of the largest invasive removal programs ever undertaken. As goat and pig populations declined, the vegetation recovered and many indigenous species have returned. Of particular concern, of course, were the habitats of the giant tortoises.

Certainly, the star attractions of the Galapagos are the tortoises, and we were carted to two sites to see them: the Giant Tortoise Reserve in the Santa Cruz highlands and the Charles Darwin Research Center on the outskirts of Puerto Ayora. The Giant Tortoise Reserve at first glance appeared to be a big grassy pasture with large boulders scattered about. When several of the boulders moved, it became evident they were not rocks, but giant tortoises. Walking among them, I could not stop staring and taking pictures. Weighing over eight hundred pounds and living over a hundred years on average, the turtles evoked a sense of reverence. From their wrinkled old heads, their ancient eyes looked up at me as if I was a child.

In contrast to the reserve, the Charles Darwin Research Center looked more like a visitor center at a national park; it contained a museum with exhibits and a breeding center. At the rearing house, after the incubation of eggs, the hatchlings and young turtles are nurtured until they are old enough for release. The enclosures held tortoises ranging from babies to several years old. The featured attraction of the center, however, was Lonesome George and his story has been told by Henry Nicholls (2006) in *Lonesome George: The Life and Loves of a Conservation Icon.* In the 16th century, as many as a quarter of a million tortoises roamed the Galapagos, but by the 1970s the numbers had dwindled to 3,000. Lonesome George was discovered as the sole survivor of one of the fifteen original subspecies of giant tortoises; ten subspecies still remain on the islands, four have become extinct, and George was the last survivor of the Isla Pinta subspecies. In the 1970s he was taken to the center for his safety but attempts to breed him were unsuccessful. In June 2012 he died at the ripe old age of between eighty and one hundred years old.

As I roamed the center, I was reminded of how important the animals of the Galapagos have been to our fundamental understanding of biology. Darwin's observations of these tortoises (as well as the islands' finches) contributed to his theory of evolution. In modern science where knowledge is gained from experimentation and the use of highly complex instruments and technology, it strikes me as remarkable that someone could make simple observations of the natural world and come up with an explanation of how life on our planet came into being and how it evolved. Observational science, what naturalists are often said to do, is not as well esteemed or deemed as relevant as the experimental sciences. Much more credibility and status is often given to the molecular biologists with their gene probes and DNA sequencers, or other scientists with their electron microscopes, telescopes, mass spectrometers, particle colliders, and seismometers. Yet in the hands (or rather, eyes and mind) of a remarkable synthesizer, the interpretation of observations was made with profound implications.

Our exploration of several of the Galapagos Islands began on a day that dawned sunny and bright. The ocean mirrored the blue cloudless sky, the white sands gleamed, the water sparkled, and it was a day in paradise. The "yacht" described in our itinerary that would take us to North Seymour Island turned out to be a 30-foot cabin cruiser. How we got twenty people on board was a feat worthy of the old phone booth packing trick college students performed in the 1950s. With life jackets strapped around us, we moved like Pillsbury doughboys, and every space in the boat seemed to be filled with orange puff as we sped away from the dock and out onto the blue waters.

The wind was calm so the ride was smooth. We anchored in a small cove and took a tiny rubber craft, holding five people at a time, onto North Seymour Island. The itinerary included a walk on a weather-bleached boardwalk that twisted and curved through the dry brush. The guide instructed us to keep on the boardwalk so as to protect the vegetation and not disturb the birds. One lady stumbled, caught the high heel of her shoe in a crack and broke it off so she limped along, someone dropped and then stepped on his sunglasses, another fellow lathering up with sunscreen slopped it all over the walkway, and yet another fellow kept swinging his gargantuan zoom camera around. With so many distractions, it was hard to concentrate and observe the surroundings, and difficult not to be annoyed at the goings-on.

The leafless palo santo trees were silver gray and had a spooky old-tree look. They are in the same family as the frankincense tree, and a local custom uses burning pieces as incense to rid a house of bad energy. In the palo santo trees, frigate birds perched and stretched their wings like black umbrellas opening and closing, and they kept rearranging their positions, with the males inflating their red pouches in courtship display. In the sky these seabirds are graceful with deeply forked tails and long sharp-edged wings that allow them to glide like kites, but in their nesting branches, they are awkward and rather clumsy. Closely related to pelicans, they have many common traits; they are fishing birds, colonial nesters, and generally raise one chick at a time. A few blue-footed boobies waddled alongside the boardwalk almost close enough to touch, their webbed feet looking as if they had been dipped in a bucket of sky.

Back to the boat and on to Santa Cruz Island, we anchored at Las Bachas and were close enough to shore to hop out of the boat. Las Bachas is a white coral sandy beach where we were able to lose the crowd for a while and walk on our own. But it seemed no sooner had we gotten there than the guide motioned for us to depart, and we were back to the boat and on to port. I was beginning to wonder if some of us humans had evolved from herd animals.

The next day's excursion on our "yacht" was to South Plaza Island. Just another day in a tropical paradise. The sky was again cloudless, the waters smooth as a polished turquoise stone, and the weather alone was enough to put me in a good mood. Sally lightfoot crabs, sporting a school team's red and yellow jerseys, scampered in all directions as we stepped off the rubber raft onto the black lava rocks. Prickly pear cactus trees (*Odonatus echios*) and a crimson ground cover (*Sesuvium* species) gave the island a Martian look, red and alien. Each tree appeared to have its own resident land iguana. Each iguana was king of its shade circle and was like a miniature dinosaur defending its territory. I was glad they were only a foot long. From a safe distance, we watched male sea lions on the rocks bellowing and grunting, exhibiting postural displays in their efforts to keep their harems in line.

We headed to the small bay, Punta Carrion, where some of our fellow travelers put on gear and snorkeled in the transparent waters. The translucent outline of rays and white-tipped reef sharks glided by and I wondered if it was such a good idea to be swimming with the sharks, but after an hour or so everyone climbed back on board, all accounted for. Then back we sped to the dock and our last evening meal.

The final morning, the lobby was teeming with people trying to checkout, and the bus was packed with sunburned faces. From the highway to the airport the rock island, Daphne Major, zoomed by as a small lump on the sea's horizon. The island was the site of Rosemary and Peter Grant's research on the Darwin finches. Jonathan Weiner in his 1995 Pulitzer Prize-winning book, *The Beak of the Finch: A Story of Evolution* (Weiner 1994), recounts how the Grants documented the process of natural selection. Returning to the island for six months of the year over a period of forty years, they observed and reported the process of natural selection. Like Darwin, through observation they noted the patterns of changes in body size and beak traits in several populations of finches, showing how natural selection could actually occur in relatively short time periods.

The bus dropped us off at the airport and we stood in a long line waiting for seat assignments. Shuffling along with the crowd onto the packed plane, I found my seat and buckled up. As the plane banked and made its way back to Quito, I looked out over the islands surrounded by the tropical blue waters and recalled that Darwin had been on the Galapagos for five weeks, where he observed and formulated his theory of natural selection and evolution. I was on the islands for only four days, where I observed and formulated my theory: there are too many of us.

CHAPTER 7.

Barrier Island: United States, Florida, Amelia Island

Barrier islands parallel the shoreline of about 13 percent of the world's coastlines, and in the U.S. they occur along the East and the Gulf Coasts. The barrier islands of North Carolina and Virginia are known as the Outer Banks; the barrier islands of South Carolina, Georgia, and Florida, are known as the Sea Islands. Of the hundreds of Sea Islands, Amelia Island is one of the southernmost, located at the border of Georgia and Florida. To the immediate south, Fort George Island has Fort George Cultural State Park, the Kingsley Plantation, Big Talbot State Park, and Little Talbot State Park. To the north, Cumberland Island is completely in conservation and is a national park, the result of efforts by many dedicated conservationists (Harlan 2014). Further north, Sapelo Island, Jekyll Island, and Hilton Head are other Sea Islands well known as vacation spots and tourist destinations.

Barrier islands function as moderators of ocean swells, and protect the wetlands situated behind them from storms. The salt marshes, among the most productive lands on earth, would not exist without barrier islands. As borderlands between the mainland and the sea, barrier islands have habitats that support unique wildlife and plants, but because they have beaches and waterways, they are popular places to live and development has occurred. Not only are barrier islands borderlands in a geological sense, they are also borderlands between environmentalists who would keep them as natural and as pristine as possible and developers who would transform them into humanscapes.

Stretching eighteen miles long, Amelia Island at its widest is three miles and has two state parks at either end, a three mile, three hundred-acre salt marsh and maritime forest called Egan's Greenway, and a number of small parks, reserves, and other protected lands. Roughly 10 percent of the island is in parks and preserves.

To escape the upstate New York winters, I rented a condo on Amelia Island for several winters and became a snowbird. My first explorations of the island began at the northern end where the town of Fernandina Beach sports an old town and historic district with restaurants, shops, bakeries, a couple of marinas, and two independent bookstores, one of which was priced out of its downtown location in 2015. The Eagan Greenway and Fort Clinch State Park are also on the northern end of the island.

My first hike along the Eagan Greenway led to an encounter with wood storks, once an endangered species, now classified only as a threatened species. Wildlife and Fisheries changed this bird's status in June of 2014 because of pressure from the Home Builders Association. In the 1930s, Florida's population of wood storks was 40,000, but by the 1970s they had declined to around 10,000, and the species was placed on the endangered species list in the 1980s. Today there are an estimated 9,000 breeding adults, many of which live in restored or artificial wetlands. There are many conservationists who believe that such small numbers did not warrant a change in status and the birds should be added once again to the endangered species list.

The storks were feeding in the backwaters of the tidal creek and before I realized it, I was within a few yards of the birds. Prehistoric, pterodactyl looking, these birds are related to the ibis, but they resemble vultures with skin heads and vulture-like posture. While these storks might not be the most attractive birds, in western culture, a related species, the white stork has always been a symbol of childbirth and in European countries, good luck. As I watched the pair dip and dredge the shallows, I was reminded that storks (there are nineteen species) don't sing; they communicate by bill clattering and it was amusing to imagine how a conversation between two birds might be just the way to click.

Located near the northern trailhead of Egan's Greenway, Fort Clinch State Park has one of the most stunning maritime forests. Spanish moss hangs from hundred-year-old live oaks that line the road into the park. The oaks form a breathtaking tunnel that runs through ancient dunes from the park's entrance to the visitor center. The dunes closest to the ocean are over thirty feet, the ones more inland are shorter and support dense native coastal vegetation. Cypress trees stand submerged in blackwater pools and holly trees speckle the sandy trails. With the red berries of the sparkleberry, yaupon, and dahoon holly, the trails in winter have a holiday Christmas feel. The spicy aroma of bay leaves baking in the sun is common, but one occasionally gets a whiff of the paper mill just north of the park. Owned by RockTenn/Rayonier, the paper company is known for its support of the local arts and makes generous contributions to the annual Amelia Island Chamber Music Festival. While the paper mill odor is not pleasant, nor are the timber trucks that roar through town, one has to consider that the mill brings four hundred and forty-one jobs (according to the company's website) and supposedly boosts the island's economy. Writing in my notebook, I am reminded that if I want paper, there must be paper mills. Yet I am always suspicious of arguments that use job creation to excuse poor environmental practices.

Near the state park are several undisturbed dunes where posted signs indicate sea turtle nesting sites. Thanks to the efforts of the Amelia Island Sea Turtle Watch, loggerheads, green sea and leatherback turtles continue to nest successfully on the island. In 2014, one hundred and sixty nesting sites were located along this nine-mile stretch of beach. Formed in 1985 with the help of Greenpeace and the Florida Department of Natural Resources, the Amelia Island Sea Turtle Watch has helped moderate the adverse impact of human activities on sea turtles. A group of about sixty volunteers conducts surveys, monitors nest sites, and has lobbied for lighting restrictions on city and county beaches during the nesting season (May through October). Sea Turtle Watch has also been responsible for a city ordinance to keep the beaches free of beach articles like canopies, cabanas, tents, and umbrellas so that turtles have free access to the dunes.

Another feature, not a sanctuary in the truest sense, is a six-mile section of the East Coast Greenway. A hard-surface trail, its most scenic section runs from Peter's Point to the Nassau Bridge and passes through a maritime forest of old live oaks and high-canopied longleaf pines. With an understory of saw palmettos and shrub magnolias, the trail accesses a longleaf pine ecosystem, once one of the most abundant habitats of the southeast coastal plain, now almost gone. The scent of pine needles baking in an afternoon sun, the salty air from the ocean, and the tangy salt marsh create one of the most pleasant smelling walks imaginable.

The southern end of the island is mostly upscale developments with gated communities, resorts and small shopping malls. The Omni Resort is one of these. Once known as Amelia Island Sea Pines Plantation, it was developed by Charles Frazier of the Sea Pines Company. John McPhee's *Encounters with the Archdruid* (1971) describes the conflict of such developers and environ-mentalists. High-end resorts like the Ritz-Carlton, the Osprey Village, the Dunes Club, the Residency, Amelia Seaside Retreat, and the Sanctuary are scattered along the southern end of the island, but across the bridge onto Little Talbot and Big Talbot

Island, public lands in the form of two state parks, Little Talbot and Big Talbot State Park, stretch along much of the coastline.

It was on Little Talbot Island that I observed my first snowy owl, and it was more accident than planning. I had pulled into the park planning to walk the trails when the park ranger asked if I was there to see the snowy owl. He gave directions to the owl's last location and suggested a safe distance from which to observe the bird. I was not alone, for when I arrived at the parking lot, six other birders and a park ranger waited with scopes and cameras, anxious to see and record this rare bird. The ranger led the group along a wooden walkway through the dunes onto the beach and found the bird perched on a piece of driftwood near the wrack line. What a sight to see this arctic bird on the white sandy beaches of Florida when its usual home is the Canadian tundra. What brought the bird down in 2014 was what is called an irruption of snowy owls. The phenomenon is cyclic and the result of fluctuations in prey populations. High populations of lemmings, voles, and other prey lead to large clutches of owl eggs, and the young birds, in search of food, move south. Snowy owl sightings were reported all along the southeastern shoreline and as far as Bermuda that year.

The bird was a young female and stood about two feet high. Largely white with lots of brown barring and spots, she moved with that typical owl head swivel, and with a regal face and yellow catlike eyes, she was majestic. To know that Little Talbot State Park was providing sanctuary to North America's largest species of owl was good reason to give thanks for Florida's state parks. To know that my sales tax dollars, real estate taxes, and trust fund monies are helping to keep these parks operating is good enough argument for everyone to pay his or her fair share of taxes.

Near Little Talbot State Park is a bird rescue and rehabilitation center known as BEAKS. Cofounder Cindy Mosling has been a bird rescuer for over thirty years, and through mostly private donations, she set up this rescue center twenty seven years ago. Her efforts have saved thousands of owls, bald eagles, herons, and other species of injured birds. BEAKS made the news in the winter of 2015 when volunteers and students saved a large number of pelicans injured in what was believed to be intentionally.

While Amelia Island has experienced extensive development with malls, shopping centers, ten golf courses, and many housing developments, it has a respectable amount of protected lands. The island is a mixture of developed land and protected lands, and while, like any environmentalist, I would wish for more land in conservation, the island compares well with islands that have long histories of conservation. Amelia Island, whose lands totals about 10 percent in conservation, compares well to Long Island, for example, which has about 15 percent. As barrier islands go, it would be encouraging if Amelia Island could have more protected areas, but given our desire for beaches and warm sunny places, that is unlikely to happen. But even with its desirability, it is an island that evokes for me a certain hopefulness with its many parks and preserves, its conservationists like Cindy Mosling, the volunteer turtle watchers, and even the tiny efforts by homeowners whose lawns are not water-demanding grass but rather native coastal flora.

CHAPTER 8.

The Flamingos of Djerba: Tunisia

I suppose I had expected to see a pristine beach on this North African shoreline of the Mediterranean Sea, but the snack wrappers, lost sandals, plastic bottles and all sorts of litter left by tourists was a disappointment. While the sun sparkled off the aquamarine waters and the sky was a cloudless blue, giving the day a bright glorious feel, the jagged edge of the high-rise hotels that lined the shore was a reminder that so many of world's shorelines have been transformed into resorts. I was traveling with a commercial tour company that offered a package deal, seven days in Tunisia for a modest price. The itinerary started from the capital, Tunis, with a brief visit to the ancient ruins of Carthage (now a modern suburb) and then on to the southern part of the country, stopping at various historical sites such as the remains of a Roman villa, a small city and a coliseum, several ancient Berber cities and their medinas, and the Sahara desert oasis of Ksar Ghilane. The island of Djerba was the final leg of the tour before returning to Tunis and home.

Legend has it that this island was the land of the lotus eaters. In Homer's Odyssey, the lotus was a flower like the water lily with mystical properties, although most historians believe what the sailors actually consumed was a fermented drink concocted from the date palm. The legend goes: Whoever eats the lotus will stay forever, feasting on them and forgetting their homeland and their responsibilities. When Odysseus' sailors started eating (or drinking), they had little incentive or interest in returning home, hence the legend. I didn't notice lotus flowers or drinks made from either the flower or the palm date, but I did enjoy the popular pale lager, Berber Blonde, and the dark beer, Stella Black, none of which lessened my desire to return home.

Earlier the first morning on the island, we visited an olive grove and watched the locals harvesting the fruit, then made a stop to an olive processing facility where the olives were pressed into olive oil. Later in the afternoon we drove along the island's shoreline where we spotted the flamingos; flamingos by the thousands feeding in the shallows of the bay, stretching as far as the eye could see, pinking the horizon. The species were the lesser and greater African flamingos and they migrate to these waters in winter from Southern Africa. Their exact migratory routes haven't been precisely worked out but these shallow bays provide excellent winter feeding grounds for the birds. About a third of all the Mediterranean flamingos migrate here to feed along this shoreline. The IUCU reports that lesser flamingos have declined by 21 to 27 percent in the last two decades and have ranked their conservation status as near-threatened. Loss of habitat and pollution are believed to be the culprit. This wetlands, part of the Migratory Bird Sanctuary also known as Djerba Bin El Quedian, has been an attempt to reverse this trend. Wetland areas have been set aside by the government of Tunisia to specifically protect flamingos. Unlike many bird sanctuaries, there were no visitor centers, no trails, no markers, no toilets, no access, no administrative staff, no infrastructure; it is simply wetlands put aside for the birds. National laws have been passed making it a crime to harm the birds, and the bay and wetlands are legally designated areas that provide them with safe haven. The birds are not a tourist attraction; they're not used to boost the economy; they are just allowed to be.

As the evening sun began to sink slowly into the sea and the water and sky turned the color of fire, a small flock of flamingos lifted off like blooming roses and flew straight as arrows toward the red target sky. For a moment, I wondered if it was more the beauty of this shoreline rather than the magic of the lotus or some mythical brew that made this island a place difficult to leave. The fact that the government of Tunisia and its people has enacted enlightened conservation policies that serve to protect threatened species of flamingos makes it a place worthy of residing.

MOUNTAINS

CHAPTER 9.

Brown Bears: Romania, Carpathian Mountains

It wasn't that I was particularly interested in vampires, although I admit to reading some of Ann Rice's *Interview with a Vampire*, watching *Buffy the Vampire Slayer*, and even reading part of one of Stephanie Meyer's *Twilight* series. I was more curious about why everyone else seemed fascinated with them. So when I saw the advertisement in my birding magazine for a tour called "Birding Transylvania," I jumped at the chance to see the region where the vampire mythology supposedly originated, and with the add-on chance of seeing brown bears and some rare birds, I was sold. I sent in my money, booked a flight, and found myself with six other birders in Budapest boarding a van to Romania.

As we crossed the Hungarian border into Romania, the road narrowed and acquired potholes. The contrast between the two countries was jolting. Old factories, run-down concrete build-ings, exposed pipelines, and power lines gave the landscape the look of an abandoned industrial zone. The roadsides were lit-tered with trash, and the villages looked scruffy. The red-tile roofs of many homes were chipped and broken and some of them sagged. Few yards had flowers, chickens ran about in the dirt, and the occasional old water well lay in ruins. In the center of towns, apartment buildings, resembling the old 1950s Soviet Union col-lectives, were plain and featureless. Only the gypsy houses looked prosperous, but they had a garish sort of glamour. Constructed as multi-storied villas surrounded in balconies, with arches and turrets, gables and towers, and ornate metal zinc roofs, they literally glittered. With metal roofs, extravagantly decorated with flowers and five-pointed and three-pointed stars enclosed in circles resembling the Mercedes Benz emblem, the villas were almost exhausting in their conspicuous and contrived designs.

Romania is about the size of Oregon, with the Carpathian Mountains forming a reverse C-shaped range in the middle of the country. In the center of the C is Transylvania, home of vampires, werewolves, and Goth. At Sighisoara, we put on our tourist hats and walked the streets around Prince Vlad Tepes' (Dracula) house in the bright sunlight of the cool autumn morning. With narrow cobblestone streets, colorful stucco apartments, red geraniums on the windowsills, high-steepled churches topped with wrought-iron crosses, brick archways, weathered tile roofs, and chimneys, the village did not seem at all in the spirit of Dracula. It had the Old World charm of a lovely medieval European city. A few visitors strolled around enjoying the pleasant morning. It would be some days before I encountered anything remotely spooky.

In Harghita County and the city of Odorheiu Secuiesi, we spent several nights exploring the mountains and alpine meadows of the area known as Szekely Land, a Hungarian term referring to the region first settled by the Huns. Our daily excursions provided fields of spotted autumn crocuses and several species of threatened and protected plants like the edelweiss (*Leontopodium alpinum*) and the yew (*Taxus baccata*). Near the village of Ivo, we came upon a rare Ural owl perched in a fir tree. Out in the open on a sunny branch, he watched us for a time while everyone oohed and aahed and clicked pictures. Moving to an open log, he slowly closed his eyes and sunned for a bit. Then suddenly as if realizing enough was enough, he opened his eyes, lifted his enormous wings, and flew back into the sanctuary of his dark forest.

Romania is about 27 percent forest and has the largest undisturbed forest in Europe. Much of the lands around Madarasi-Hargita Mountain are protected, and some of the thirty-six protected areas and national parks have large stands of virgin spruce, fir, and beech. In search of brown bears one evening, we drove to one of the conservation areas. Small wooden sheds had been erected to offer camouflaged viewing. About six feet off the ground, the blinds provide an elevated observation point. At the edge of the clearing, small offerings of peanut butter and fruit were put out to entice the bears. When we started the trek to the bear blinds, there was still daylight enough to see, but it was not an easy trail. The ground was wet, uneven, and full of roots, ruts, and puddles. Even though a thick carpet of pungent and tangy-smelling spruce needles covered the ground, the trail was treacherous.

As we slogged along toward the blinds, two bears suddenly rushed from out of the deep woods. The larger bear lumbered out in front of me about twenty yards ahead and the smaller one scuttled behind me. It happened so quickly, I was terrified for only a moment, realizing that I was between two bears, probably a mother and her cub. They were black shadows, gone before I could really get a good look, and they faded like ghosts into the dusky forest in an instant. No one had time to register the fact that these were the bears we had come to see. I guess someone forgot to tell the bears to wait until we were in the blinds.

The organization responsible for the bear blinds, the Carpathian Wildlife Foundation, estimates there are a little over 6,000 brown bears in the region. Organizations such as the European Union, World Wildlife Fund, European Nature Trust, and Carpathian Large Carnivore Project have been instrumental in conserving bear habitats, and bear populations have been increasing. The Carpathian brown bear is a protected species, and ecotours have increased bear awareness. The ecology of these animals, like most species of *Ursus,* reveals an omnivore although bears in general are considered carnivores (Slobodyan 1976). The brown bear's actual diet consists mostly of plant matter, but almost anything edible can provide nutrition. A wild pig's skin was discovered in the stomach of one dead bear, and remains of a young sheep and roe deer were found in two others. Brown bears hibernate from October/December to March/May and forage hundreds of kilometers during the autumn to find food and build up fat before hibernating. They live solitary lives except in mating season in May/June and generally have two cubs in January. Cubs remain with their mother for three or four years; they mature sexually at around four to six years; and they live on average twenty to thirty years. The largest Romanian bear was recorded at over 1,050 pounds.

As we settled into the blinds, we hoped the bears would return, but after several hours of no show we gave up and walked back to the vans. The forest by now was a black hole. The guides had one tiny flashlight and we walked blind. Strange noises surrounded us, but I told myself it was only the sucking sound of our boots in the marshy ground. The trail was impossible to see and the pinpoint dot of a flashlight bouncing around like a firefly was hardly a guiding light. I began to understand why Bram Stoker set his 1897 Gothic novel *Dracula* in Transylvania. It was really spooky. I expected any minute to bump into a bear, to hear "the howls of wolves," or see "mysterious blue flames appearing in the dark," or maybe brush against a bat up to no good.

That evening after dinner an educational film provided by the lodge offered some explanations regarding the Dracula myth. Several historians claimed an outbreak of rabies occurred during that time and some of the wolves and bats of the region had become rabid. Although animal attacks were numerous, a local ruler, Vlad Tepes (known as the Impaler), may have been the target on which to place the blame. The film suggested a viral disease and a fifteenth-century wacko prince as the origin of the vampire myth. It gets even a little more confusing because the actual historical record suggests Vlad Tepes may have been a "good tyrant," but the Dracula-as-terror myth brings so much tourist money that Romanians have been somewhat reluctant to dispel the bloodthirsty legends. Although the film was informative, it didn't really answer my question, "Why are we so attracted to vampires?" As archetypal figures vampires represent danger, power, the erotic, and immortality, and I imagine one might argue that these are compelling elements. Mary Hallab (2009) in *Vampire God: The Allure of the Undead in Western Culture* suggests that our infatuation with vampires allows us to consider death without really facing it. I suppose that's as good a reason as any, but sometimes I wonder if it's just that vampires seem to have such an interesting sense of fashion.

The next morning at 2:30 a.m., we left the city, drove two and a half hours on washboard roads, and climbed in the dark for several hours up a steep mountain trail to see the rare capercaillie. I opted out of the climbing part because of a respiratory infection and crawled into the back of the van to catch a few more z's while the others trekked up the mountainside. Six hours later they returned—cold, worn out, and a little disappointed at having seen the birds as tiny dark specks far off in the distance. But no one complained when we passed around the breakfast bags. The British birders were especially quiet as they gulped down every crumb of their breakfast. British birders make us Americans look like sissies. We Americans tend to fret and complain if things get a bit uncomfortable, but the Brits are tough as nails. One of the members of our band of birders was a tiny 80-year-old lady bent over with osteoporosis. She had been a birder most of her life. She never tired, she never complained, and she could walk circles around us younger folks. After that cold climb and long unrewarding watch, she remarked, "Well, wasn't that a jolly good morning!" and she meant it.

The last leg of our tour in Romania was an afternoon of meadow walking and an overnight in the quaint village of Torocko, a

UNESCO World Heritage site, also called Rimetea. The buildings of the village are centuries old, and its citizens are trying to restore and maintain the rural nature of the town. Our hosts provided us with a hearty dinner, bringing out mounds of baked potatoes, platters heaped with steaming pork roast, and lots of homemade plum brandy. After dinner we stumbled off to our rooms wishing each other affectionate good nights, probably the effect of the brandy. The next morning the ride back to Hungary was sort of a blur, possibly the wearing-off of the brandy, but later in the afternoon, when my thoughts became more coherent, I recalled the places we had visited. I still had no clue why vampires have such appeal or why there is so much interest in them, but I did learn that there is a lot of interest in bears, real bears, and a good deal of interest in protecting them. The parks and preserves, the protected lands, the UNESCO sites are all attempts at preserving the bear's habitat as well as the country's natural and historical places. The most hopeful message of the trip was that some folks are spending their time and energy preserving a past, not one based on creatures of fear and terror but a past based on sound ecology and preservation. Yet maybe if stretched a bit, one might also imagine that even vampires, as tourist attractions, are helping to save the bears.

CHAPTER 10.

The Abyssinian Wolf: Ethiopia, Bale Mountain National Park

My fondest memory of Ethiopia was having my hand kissed. Our group was birding near Debre Libanos in the Jemma Valley over-looking an escarpment whose view could easily rival the U.S. Grand Canyon. The multicolored rock walls plunged a mile deep into a gorge with the Jemma River at the bottom. The cliffs were the colors of caramel, latte, creamed corn, and tomato soup, and the river below was a silver thread weaving its way to the Blue Nile. Our meager lunch of a boiled egg and a dry cheese sand-wich may have been the reason the rock colors looked so delec-table. After that sparse meal, I made my way to the toilet, a small mud hut built on a concrete slab where a cleaning woman was busy mopping. Barefoot and wearing a loose-fitting gray skirt and gray rag wrapped around her head, she sloshed a heavy mop back and forth. Splashing water from the bucket over the floor, she scrubbed with such effort that it seemed her sole pur-pose in life was to keep that floor clean. I returned to my lunch spot, checked my backpack, and came back with a fifty-birr note (about five dollars). When I slipped the bill into her hand, she looked at it in astonishment. She seized my hand in her rough callused ones and kissed it gently, mumbling a string of words I assumed were thanks. Her astonishment left her smooth obsid-ian face and attached itself to mine. I had never experienced such a tactile expression of gratitude. I bowed "you're welcome" and returned to the cliffs where my fellow travelers were pitching scraps to the kites and vultures. The huge birds dove and soared, swooping close to the cliff edge, scooping up the thrown morsels like greedy gulls. Lunch break ended as a troop of gelados baboons meandered in the rocks below, climbed up the cliffs, and disappeared over the rim. As we drove away from the gorge, I smiled at the cleaning woman's exaggerated good-bye waves. It was early in the trip and little did I know this encounter would be one of my few pleasurable moments.

The afternoon we arrived in the capital, Addis Ababa, the streets were full of armed troops. On every street corner, men in faded blue and white camouflage stood with rifles slung over their shoulders. The U.S. news was full of reports about the unrest in this part of the world: to the north, Sudan and Darfur; to the south, Kenya with the surges of "ethnic cleansing" directed against the Kikuyu by anti-Kikuyu factions; to the west, Somalia; and to the east, Eritrea, with its border disputes with Ethiopia. But I believed the region around the capital where we would be traveling was stable, so it was disturbing to see so many heavily armed soldiers and I wondered just how safe our journey was going to be. We later learned the troops were security for the African Union Conference being held in the city, and the next day when the conference came to an end, the troops left, and the city returned to a more relaxed, less militaristic mood.

After two days in Addis and some rather disagreeable events—a vehicle breakdown on the way back to our lodging after a long day in the field, a filthy hotel room where from the window, a raw loose electric wire danced and sparked blue flashes all night long, and an unpleasant reprimand from our guides because we complained—we left the city. Our five jeeps crammed full of twice as many travelers as claimed in the tour company's brochure bounced along toward Afar country. "Driving in Ethiopia is not an easy experience," wrote Pico Iyer (2007: 21).

He certainly had that observation right. Even more troublesome than the rough roads was the lodging that offered little in the way of relief at the end of the day. Amenities such as hot water for showers, electricity, and food without too much spice were scarce. In Addis our guides had insisted we try injera, a large gray spongy pancake with the texture of a reusable air conditioner filter. The injera, or more likely, the wat, the spicy stews sopped up with the injera, put my digestive tract into an uproar, and every day it got worse.

This same Ethiopian birding tour was described by Alan Davies and Ruth Miller (2010) in *The Biggest Twitch: Around the World in 4,000 Birds*. These authors recount their adventures as they traveled the world in an attempt to break the record of most birds seen in one year (which they did). When I first read their description of this tour, I was reminded of the Japanese film Rashomon, which tells the tale of a murder through the narratives of five different people and reveals the slippery nature of truth, the complexity of experience, and the diversity of perceptions. Each person's rendition of the events in that story was different, and so it was with my experience of Ethiopia, which differs from these authors. While Ruth and Alan were the kindest and most considerate of our fellow travelers, sharing their scope and pointing out bird species in a manner both gracious and apt, which made their rendition of the tour a bit more acceptable, it was still a surprise to see the tour portrayed as an exciting adventure. I am more inclined to define the trip as an expensive endurance test.

From the Jemma River Gorge we made our way through the Rift Valley to Awash. Ethiopia's Rift Valley has been called "The Great Fossil Field" because of the many archaeological discoveries made there. Probably the most celebrated was of the remains of the early hominid "Lucy" (Johanson and Edey 1981) in the 1970s. Since that time continual findings in the region have pushed the origins of humans back to over four million years, with the unearthing of the bipedal fossil named "Ardi," a shortened name for the genera of early hominids *Ardipthecus*; and even further back to possibly six million years, with the findings of evidence of stone tool making. Our caravan pulled off on a roadside clearing for a leg-stretch where we encountered a fellow who could easily have been a relative of *Australopithecus afarensis*. This Afar warrior was an exotic looking fellow in his thin leather sandals and white clothing draped over a lean ebony body. The well oiled, AK47 rifle slung over his shoulder added another intriguing element to his attire. After a brief exchange between him and our guides, we left him our empty plastic water bottles, which seem to be a useful commodity in a region where sources of water are scarce. As we drove off into the arid red plains toward our next stop, he disappeared in a cloud of rusty dust.

Later that evening we arrived in Metehara, a bustling village whose main street was lined with tin sheds and shacks. It was good to be off the road after so many jostling hours where trucks whose cargo ranged from camels to soda pop zoomed at breakneck speed, weaving in and out of the narrow lanes until the only relief was to just stop looking. A walk along a nearby alkaline lake was a welcome relief after the day's drive. Only later did I learn that the lake was full of crocodiles and that recently a visitor had been attacked and killed by a hungry croc.

That night my gastroenteritis got worse. Crossing a railroad track to a cafe for dinner, a sudden wave of nausea and diarrhea hit. I looked desperately for somewhere to squat, but there was nothing but a cluster of small thorn bushes near the corner of a shed, so that's where I headed. Because it was almost dark, no one was shocked at coming across an old woman squatting in the bushes. Getting thorn spikes in my behind was bad enough, but when my traveling companion had an even worse attack of gastritis, threw up, and passed out later that evening, our health was becoming a little more concerning.

My traveling companion revived, fell into a deep sleep, and seemed to be all right the next day, but a restful night was not in the cards. Gunshots rang out all night long and the next morning our guides reported a shoot-out at the train station when the police confiscated contraband from a group of smugglers on the train. The contraband was not drugs or guns but music tapes and DVDs, really dangerous stuff.

In Ethiopia with a Mule, Irish traveler writer Dervla Murphy (1968) describes a three-month, 900-mile trek through northern Ethiopia in the 1960's. She suffered robberies, intense sunburn, scratches from thorn bushes that turned infectious, falls, dysentery, and bites from mosquitoes, flies, bees, and leeches. Constantly drinking a local fermented brew called talla, Murphy endured extreme discomforts. It is not quite clear whether the harsh conditions caused the beer consumption or if the local brew caused some of the discomfort, but I do know that I consumed a lot of beer on the trip and would highly recommend the practice.

Having recovered from her bout of gastroenteritis, my traveling companion joined the group for a visit to the Awash National Park, but I was still too dizzy and nauseated so I remained in the grimy hotel room trying to get my bearings. The noise blaring from the mosques' loudspeakers all day long did not make for a restful day, however, and I was more than ready to move on the next morning. On the road again for another long stretch of rough riding, we arrived at a lodge full of German tourists who were traveling in a big red sleeper bus. If someone had said I would see a busload of festive Germans bouncing along the African plains, I would not have believed it, but there they were as zany as a scene from the movie, "The Adventures of Priscilla, Queen of the Desert."

Birding in the acacia forest around the lodge was a stroll through a tintype landscape. The leafless trees were sepia, the ground was tawny, and the lacy shadows cast by the branches were shoe polish brown. Termite mounds the shape of sand castles and the color of peanut butter dotted the forest floor. Teardrop shaped weaver bird nests hung from low branches, and in other trees, huge globular nests—concatenations of sticks and straw—filled the crotches. The nests belonged to several species of social weaver bird. One of the guides told a story of a young woman whose thesis was a study of these birds. She had a protective hand and arm shield made so she could reach in, collect, and count the chicks. The shield was to protect her from snakes that enter the nest and eat the eggs and chicks (nearly 70 percent of all weaver bird chicks are eaten by snakes). A former student had not been so careful and when he began to explore the nests, he was bitten by a Cape cobra and died a painful death. Such stories did not relieve my anxiety about walking these grounds.

The drive to Bale Mountain National Park involved another two days of rough terrain with an overnight at a lodge located on a mountaintop. We arrived at the mountain lodge after sunset, so the quarter-mile climb in the dark on a narrow trail, whose partial wooden railing was more trail marker than safety feature, was a heart stopper. How we made it up that mountain in the dark without mishap still remains a mystery. No electricity meant cold showers, and tasteless food made for an unsatisfying evening, but the beer was exceptionally cold having been left outside in the cold mountain temperature. The frigid air made for a bitterly cold night, and I ended up putting on in my heaviest pants, fleece jacket and other clothing at various intervals throughout the night. By daybreak I was wrapped up like a cocoon barely able to move.

The following day was another long ride through mountainous terrain with miles of road construction and delays. It would have been a beautiful drive, as the landscape was beautiful highland forests, but many of the old alpine trees were being cut. Huge ancient trees lay felled along the wide swath of roadbed. The road was being built by Chinese workers as a project funded by China to improve the country's infrastructure, and whose purpose was to open transportation between the wheat-growing plains and Addis, the capital. It was probably a progressive economic project, but it was disheartening to see so many of the old trees being destroyed. Upon arrival at the town of Goba and the Goba Wabe Hotel, the first thing everyone celebrated was hot water aplenty!

The morning was cool and crisp as the jeeps climbed from the Sanetti plain nearly 14,000 feet up onto the summit. The barren landscape was sparsely vegetated with giant lobelia, a few woody shrubs, dry grasses, and dusky gray lichens covering the rocks. Colonies of giant mole rats whose burrows looked like those of prairie dogs were scattered about in patches. Occasionally a rodent would pop up, look around, and run from one burrow to another.

From the right side of the jeep what appeared to be a small red fox trotted across the plain. Nose to the ground, concentrating, she was hunting. She stopped, shivered a little, then leaped into the air, came down and began digging. Dirt flew in all directions. Suddenly her head went deep into the crevice and she pulled up a wiggling rat in her jaws. She gulped the animal down and moved on to another mound. Bouncing up like a pop-up, then down with a thump, then digging, she repeated the movement again and again, catching one rat after another, which she deposited beneath nearby rocks as cache.

The Abyssinian wolf (also known as the Simien fox or the Ethiopian wolf or jackal, *Canis simensis*) is the rarest canid in the world. Conservationists estimate there are about two hundred to five hundred left in the world. A small population exists in the Simien Mountains, and the remainder live here in the Bale Mountains (Burrard et al, 2013). Not only was there something special about seeing an animal so rare, but this fox had the added quality of being sleek and beautiful.

In a remarkable story of conservation, an emergency response team of veterinarians, scouts and staff of EWCP (the Ethiopian Wolf Conservation Program) set into place a vaccination program, which probably saved these animal from extinction. In 2014 rabies was detected in a wolf carcass and the threat of rabies became a real possibility that could have resulted in the eradication of the species. In a seven-month period, the team captured and vaccinated one-third of the population (over one hundred wolves) and averted a possible outbreak of the deadly virus. The quick and effective action of these dedicated conservationists in all likelihood saved this species from extinction.

In hopes of seeing wattled cranes, two of the guides and several of our birders took off across the open plain, but the high altitude was too much for me. As much as I wanted to see these endangered birds, I could barely walk a few feet without gasping for breath so I sat in the jeep while the more rugged members of our group took off in search of cranes. An hour later they came straggling back looking like plane crash survivors. No crane sightings or any other birds for their efforts, but they were obviously relieved to have lunch and even more so, water. In the high altitude dehydration can quickly become a problem and no one had thought to take enough water in the haste to seek these birds.

Traveling once again through the Rift Valley, we made our way to Lake Awassa where in the town of Wondo Genet we lodged in small cottages along the lake. The reed beds that lined the shore provided lovely lake views. One morning as the sunrise washed the lake in soft pastels, the sight of a tiny lone boy standing on his skiff, spear in hand ready for the day's catch, had the sweet element of enchantment. But it was the fish market that made the most lasting impression. Fishing boats not much bigger than large canoes brought in the day's catch and were lined up along shore with young local boys helping to sort and process the fish. Fish guts dripping blood and smelling awful were thrown into the water, attracting hordes of white pelicans, long-tailed cormorants, marabou storks, and gulls by the hundreds. The birds grabbed and snatched the fish remains in a constant free-for-all. Feathers flew and fights broke out. It began to feel even more like a circus of beggars when gangs of small boys roamed the market mobbing us with their outstretched hands out asking for money. It was all rather overwhelming.

The next day and final drive back to Addis Ababa through the lake region was pleasant enough. The roads were good, the hotel in Addis was clean and amenable, and the flight home uneventful. What I learned from Ethiopia was probably as much about myself as the country and its conservation efforts, and while self-knowledge can be enlightening, it can sometimes be humbling. I learned that I am far too sensitive to physical discomforts; I am not very brave; I am intolerant of those who treat elderly women as an annoyance; and I am unforgiving of those who believe their games (to see a rare bird) are more crucial than courtesy and politeness. I'm not suggesting that birding isn't a legitimate activity, but it is not an excuse for disrespectful behavior. To discover my own behavior deteriorating and my sense of humor vanishing was bad enough, but to recognize that my personality was not at all the "stiff-upper-lip" was disappointing. Don't we all want to be the good guys in our stories and how disconcerting when we are not. While I applaud the Bale Mountain National Park as a place of sanctuary for the Abyssinian wolf, what I discovered in Ethiopia was that it is difficult to be compassionate, kind, tolerant or any of those admirable qualities when you're sick, in pain and uncomfortable, and when those you must depend on may have agendas other than your comfort and maybe even your safety, in mind. I did not experience Ethiopia as the country depicted in the exquisitely written novel *Cutting for Stone* (Verghese 2011), perhaps not because of the country but perhaps because of my own discomfort. It occurred to me that a sanctuary might function in the same way as caring and reliable traveling companions. If a refuge provides a safe, healthy, and comfortable place where a species can be the best that it can be, that may be one of the essential qualities of a sanctuary. The conservationists who often endure physical discomforts and hardships but are still able to create and maintain sanctuaries may be the real heroes in this world that so often feels like the fish market of Lake Awassa.

CHAPTER 11.

Mayan Ruins, Fincas, and a Quetzal: Guatemala

The flight from Tikal to Guatemala City was the last one of the day. The small plane holding ten passengers took off with the sun slipping below the horizon and a storm coming in from the south. In the cockpit, the pilot, a young man who looked barely out of his teens wore a leather flying cap, bomber jacket, gloves, and chrome RAF goggles. I thought, Snoopy. He held onto the yoke with both hands in a white-knuckle grip. He could have been outrunning the Red Baron instead of the approaching storm. Out the window huge thunderheads billowed and jags of lightning streaked down. The clouds coalesced into great golden temples with orange columns and rosy pediments. The entire sky was a palette of fiery colors streaked with dark storm clouds. The plane swayed and bounced and would occasionally roll, pause, and drop, catch, and then stabilize. The kid-pilot kept just ahead of the storm, but it was still a rough ride and I was a little surprised how calm I was. My thoughts kept drifting back to my friend who had just died after a long struggle with cancer. The day we left Guatemala City, I had gotten an email saying she had passed away. As we pitched and rolled in that tiny plane, I thought, death, where so many of my friends had gone of late, might not be such a bad place to go.

We had flown into Flores and spent three days in the Mayan

Biosphere Reserve, a six-million-acre reserve established in the 1990s by the Guatemalan government and UNESCO. The reserve is 10 percent of Guatemala's total land area and represents the largest tropical forest in Central America. Zoned into three regions, it includes the core zones at 36 percent, which encompass the parks—including the pre-Columbian Mayan city of Tikal declared a UNESCO World Heritage Site in 1979 where no settlement, no logging, and no extraction activities are allowed; the multi-use zones at 40 percent; and the buffer zones at 24 percent, which allow sustainable harvesting of wood and traditional forest products, and farming. This type of conservation, known as the nesting doll approach, represents UNESCO's practical solution to protecting many wilderness lands (Conservation Magazine 2015, Ward and Green 2015). However, monitored by the international Forest Stewardship Council, the Rainforest Alliance reports that the forest has shrunk by 13 percent in twenty-one years due to illegal logging, farming, ranching, drug trafficking, and the poaching and looting of Mayan artifacts. Because of limited resources, salaries for guards and park rangers, its wilderness location and size, it is a formidable task to protect such a reserve.

The landscape around Flores was undulating forested hills. The topography known as karst consisted of mounds and sinkholes, hills and ridges, the result of the erosion and weathering of the rock base limestone. From Flores to Tikal through a lush green terrain, the road was a rollercoaster ride. The village of El Remate provided a lakeside view of Lake Peten Itza, a breakfast of papaya and watermelon, and a walk through the protected area known as Cerro Cahuí. The moist forest reserve had many species of warblers, but the most intriguing birds were the squirrel and pheasant cuckoos. These large birds rustled along the ground among the tangles of vines and vegetation, foraging like turkeys, and to get even a glimpse, we had to do some major bending and stretching.

Arriving at Tikal we settled into the Jungle Lodge for the evening and the next morning were up at dawn. The entrance to the park still shrouded in morning fog was a short walk from the lodge. Brown jays flinging themselves from tree branch to tree branch, dragging their long tails like dark scarves, were as noisy and rancorous as all jays tend to be. Flycatchers, tanagers, and toucans were all flashes of color in the dawn's early foggy light. As the sky lightened and the fog lifted, the enormous kapok tree (*Ceiba pentandra*) that greeted every visitor entering the park was transformed from an etching into a real live barked bare-leafed tree.

We meandered the park trails the entire day stepping over leaf-cutter ants and squeezing through holes in the branches and vines of the understory. From temple to temple, altar to stela, ball court to courtyard, tomb to tomb, we rambled among the crenellated pyramids. The highest temple, number IV, offered wooden steps and a windy stairway so we climbed and stood for a while on a narrow ledge overlooking a sea of treetops. Off in the distance four other temples peeked up from the jungle as the cool breeze brought relief from the heat and humidity of ground level. Back on the trails, we continued to roam, finally ending up at the Grand Plaza, which was buzzing with tourists. We rested on stones at the edge of the plaza and observed the many surrounding buildings. In a patina that resembled tarnished silver, the temples, monuments, and palaces (there are over 3,000 structures in the city) were etched with lichens and age. Some of the emblems or glyphs were obvious while others had faded into obscurity. Hundreds of people milled about, some feeding the ocellated turkeys that begged for handouts, some chasing little kids who chased the turkeys and everyone clicking with cameras. With turquoise skin heads covered in orange-yellow bead-like nodules and eye-spots on their tails, the turkeys could have been peacocks. Their iridescent bronze and green feathers shimmered when they stuttered, and I thought these birds certainly make our American turkeys look like Plain Janes.

Ruins always evoke for me thoughts of how people lived in the past. Over a thousand years ago Tikal supported a population of 120,000 during the Classical Mayan Age and then it collapsed. Theories as to why this happened have suggested disease, political corruption, war, and food and water shortages. As a line of ants worked their way around the base of our stone steps, I wondered why so many human civilizations had risen and fallen in our short time as the dominant species on earth, and if the ants, which have been around a lot longer, might have a better handle on what makes organizations work. But I needed to be careful using such analogies, and reminded myself that even the benign plant-loving leafcutters will mercilessly kill other ant colonies near them, a trait that is clearly not what we humans should probably strive for. Guatemala has been a country where a lot of killing has occurred as is true in other Central American countries, so I suppose maybe we aren't that much different from the ants after all.

The following day a visit to another ruin, Yaxha, was a much different experience; there were few visitors and it had the feel of a real nature preserve. It was more open and free of undergrowth and its temples were not as extensive as those of Tikal, but it was quieter and more congruent with the atmosphere of a ruin, until a troop of howler monkeys came swinging through. As they roared their way among the branches, the noise and commotion was deafening. After their raucous display of branch shaking and howling, the troop moved on and the afternoon became silent again, quiet as a tomb.

Before leaving the region we explored Flores, crossing the causeway onto Flores Island and stopping at the village of St. Elena to meander the streets. Among the hotels and restaurants of the old town, a small church offered a quiet sanctuary. I lit a candle for my friend and left a small donation. It was a sad little church in need of much repair and the donation seemed somewhat futile, but perhaps in keeping with my friend's valiant struggle against great odds, it was the gesture that mattered. After our brief visit to Flores, we headed for the airport to catch the evening flight back to Guatemala City.

The second leg of the tour was from Guatemala City to the highlands and a coffee finca located on the southern slopes of the volcano Atitlan. From the main highway, a steep and narrow dirt road climbed the mountain and we bumped along for miles until the road finally ended at Los Andes. The white stucco house was shaded by palms and surrounded by lush tropical plants. Gardens of canna lilies, hostas, hibiscus, lantana, hyacinths, bougainvillea and many other flowers I did not recognize were blooming, but it was the view overlooking the volcano Toliman that was the most thrilling. It was late afternoon when we arrived and having traveled most of the day, we decided a nap before dinner would be in order. As I lay my head down on the still pillow, the rain started. It began as a light sprinkle then picked up until the beat became a kettledrum, then a deluge. Its rumble blocked out every other sound—the clanging of the staff fixing dinner, the bird calls, the insect buzzes—all noises vanished into the steady beat of the rain. Falling asleep to rain in a dry cozy bed, what more comforting a place for dreams? When I woke, the rain had stopped and I had dreamed of my friend who had just died. She was sitting on a bench in her hometown park wearing a yellow sun-dress with three friends. Everyone was licking ice cream cones. I gave thanks to rain dreams that offered the hope for a better place, a sanctuary, for her, a place more pleasant than where she had last been.

Olga Hazard said the heavy rains were common this time of year, even in February, the dry season. I could only imagine what they must be like in the rainy season. Olga and her husband, Jim, were the owners of Los Andes having purchased it in 1985. Their website describes its history at http://www.andescloudforest.org and gives a brief description of their conservation efforts. As members of a group of twenty-plus coffee growers and private nature preserves called Asociación de Reservas Naturales Privadas de Guatemala, the Hazards are committed to conservation and sustainability. They have put into practice habitat conservation and sustainability policies, keeping some land in natural forest and preserve, as well as making a commitment to the villagers who work on the land.

The next morning one of the farmhands drove us, and Juice, our guide, up the mountain for a bird walk down. With the clouds lifting off the treetops in whirly white streamers and the sun rising above the mountain, the term "cloud forest" seemed right. We stood in a clearing and watched the fruit trees in the distance as orioles, trogons, and even a motmot moved in and out. Then we began the slow walk down. At the quetzal reserve we left the road and made a wide loop through the dense forest. Juice in his rubber boots and machete led the way through the green tangles where shafts of light cut through the canopy and fell on a multitude of vines that swarmed the trees. Lianas, woody creepers, strangler figs, leafy epiphytes, and bromeliads grew in a green tapestry that seemed as tightly woven as a high-thread-count carpet. The reserve was part of the land set aside and described by Anne LaBastille in the 1960s (LaBastille, 1980). It was the first area in Guatemala officially declared for the protection of the quetzal.

A short distance into the reserve, we paused, listened, and looked around. A male quetzal perched on a nearby branch as if waiting for us to come and admire him. The bird was splendid even in the dim light. Jonathan Evan Maslow's (1986) description of the quetzal in his travelogue of Guatemala, *Bird of Life, Bird of Death: A Naturalist's Journey through a Land of Political Turmoil*, certainly did the bird justice. The iridescent green and blue—depending on how the light hit its back and head—the long tail feathers, and the red belly and breast was plumage of spectacular proportion. He didn't stay long enough and too soon flew off into the dark jungle.

Back on the main road two rare azure-rumped tanagers romping in a mahogany tree completed our findings; it was indeed a lucky morning of rare and beautiful birds. We spent the afternoon visiting the school where the village children sang for us (children whose parents work for Los Andes must attend school until at least the fourth grade), the clinic where the visiting doctor told of his public health programs, and a walk through the coffee/tea processing facility. The time went by quickly and we were soon sitting once again at the dinner table enjoying the delicious soup, grilled chicken, potatoes, and beets, all fresh from the garden and coop.

From Los Andes we traveled to Antigua where we stayed several days enjoying the sights of this old colonial city surrounded by volcanoes. The columns and arches of the palacios, the ornate rickrack of old churches, the festive music of the central plaza and the colorful markets, all made for a delightful few days. A visit to Finca El Pilar, a coffee plantation belonging to the family of Maria Rivera, owner of Kuk Tours who had put together our tour, was on the agenda for one of the days. The morning was cool and pleasant as our driver hauled us up the mountain and dropped us off near the top. Before our trek down, we watched Volcan de Fuego belch and blow a few small puffs of clouds into the blue sky. A short distance down the road, we entered the nature trail built by Maria's brother, Juan Rivera. A remarkable series of wooden steps and planks, it wound down several miles through a cloud forest providing spectacular views of treetops, deep jungled gorges, and gullies covered with dense vegetation. Reaching the bottom, we lunched with the hummingbirds as they buzzed and whizzed around the feeders.

The last day in Antigua was a drive to Panajachel on the shore of Lake Atitlán. Many years ago, I had read and admired Anne LaBastille's (1990) *Mama Poc; An Ecologist's Account of the Extinction of a Species*, which described her efforts to save the Atitlán grebe (also known as the giant grebe) from extinction. She discovered that two invasive species of bass introduced to promote fishing tourism were decimating the bird populations. In the 1960s the population was estimated at between eighty and two hundred, but their numbers were rapidly declining. In an effort to stop the decline, LaBastille tried to create a refuge and the population leveled off at 210. A devastating earthquake in the 1970s altered the lake level and the birds' habitat was dealt the final blow, driving the species over the brink into extinction. By 1989 only two birds were left and after that year none were ever sighted again. The species was deemed extinct. LaBastille's account was one of the first ecological studies documenting in detail how a species goes extinct.

To say the highway to Panajachel was heavily congested with traffic is an understatement. Chicken buses, as they are called, which are yellow Bluebird school buses painted vivid reds, blues, yellows, oranges, black, and silver, packed the road. Diesel trucks carrying heavy cargo and gazillions of cars filled the lanes. Every vehicle seemed to be spewing smoke or soot. Slowdowns were common as construction crews repaired mudslides and cave-ins from the recent rains. It took most of the morning to reach the lake.

The village of Panajachel was also congested. The narrow streets full of people were so different from what Anne LaBastille described in the 1960s (LaBastille 1990: 33). She wrote of a small village with a few houses on a quiet lake. Today, Panajachel, with its population of nearly 12,000, its hotels and resorts, its streets lined with shops, was a changed place. After walking through the large craft market full of tourists where short, black-haired Mayan women in their native huipiles looking like colorful threads woven into straw baskets hawked their wares, we had lunch at one of the hotels overlooking the lake.

The lake was as calm as a mirror and deep cerulean. The volcanoes rimming the lake made for a misty blue edge. The beauty of the lake was still as enchanting as LaBastille's original description. The disappearance of the grebe which she documented in the 1960s is a phenomenon now happening all over the world and the book's message is clear: with development comes the loss of vulnerable species. While we humans keep increasing our numbers, the other species of the world are disappearing. The idea that development brings jobs and prosperity and that it lifts people out of poverty is a myth. Clearly, some people are lifted from poverty when it occurs, but there is a cost. If the cost is the demise of certain species and the devastation of the environment, is development really worth it? The pertinent issue of how we end poverty without destroying our environment seems to be one of the most relevant questions of modernity. And it did not escape my awareness that as I sat in this hotel looking out on Lake Atitlán, I was part of the paradox.

I remembered that Guatemala had gone through a devastating civil war in the 1980s, if civil war is actually the correct term. Called genocide by some, the war destroyed hundreds of Mayan villages and killed 200,000 people, mostly Mayans. In the 1980s, Amnesty International called Guatemala the worst human rights violator in the Western Hemisphere. In 1992 Rigoberta Menchu, a member of the K'iche Maya ethnic group, was the first indigenous woman to win a Nobel Prize for her work in the area of social justice, indigenous rights, and ethno-cultural reconciliation. Her narrative as recorded and edited by Elisabeth Burgos-Debray (Menchu and Burgos-Debray 1984) describes life in the time of the violence and presents an account of the how the poor fared in Guatemala. Jonathan Evan Maslow (1986) also gives an excellent picture of the country in the 1980s when he traveled as a naturalist in search of the quetzal, and his portrayal of the terrible poverty and mistreatment of the native population is at times chilling.

Because I was returning to the cold of a New York February and the memorial service of my friend, I was reluctant to leave.

Guatemala would stay with me in memory as a country with many sanctuaries, a place where coffee plantations served as nature preserves and where social justice offered native people work and safety, a place where its national park built on ancient ruins was also a flora and fauna sanctuary, and a country where efforts to preserve its biological heritage were being actualized. It seemed Guatemala, like its sanctuaries, was a country moving toward a better place.

CHAPTER 12.

The Yungas, the Chaco, and the Altiplano:
Argentina, Salta and the Northwest

As evening spread its maroon quilt over the sky, and blue and white swallows began their aerial waltz, we sat on the Clarks' porch with Ricardo, Patricia, and their son, Mauricio, sipping maté. An herbal tea high in caffeine, vitamins, and antioxidants, maté comes from a holly known as yerba maté (*Ilex paraguariensis*) and tastes a little like green tea. The earthen-colored maté bowl was passed around and everyone sipped from the metal straw. The bowl completely enclosed the steamy tea, as too much air changes the flavors, Mauricio explained, and we passed it on from one pair of cupped hands to another. The sharing of maté, the national drink of Argentina, is a traditional social event believed to bond those who share it in eternal friendship.

We had spent the day in the Reserva del Huaico, the private one hundred and thirty-acre preserve owned by the Clarks (http://www.reservadelhuaico.org.ar/en/conservacion.php).
Their family home sits in one corner of the reserve and from the slope of Mount Huasancho overlooks the Lerma Valley. Outside the village of San Lorenzo about five miles from Salta in the foothills of the Andes, the reserve is administered through the Foundation Yuchan (an NGO or non-government, not for profit, private organization), and the Clarks have maintained the prop-

erty as a native or natural yunga habitat. With much of the area around Salta becoming pastureland for cattle or cropland for soybean and sugar, they have worked to preserve this unique and disappearing habitat.

We walked the trails and discovered that a yunga is a temperate cloud forest. The lower section of the reserve, around 4,500 feet in elevation, was a montane deciduous forest consisting of larger trees such as ceibo (*Erythrina falcata*), tipa (*Tipuana tipu*), pacara (*Enterolobium contortisiliqum*), nut tree (*Juglans australis*), and cedro (*Cedrela lilloi*). Cut by deep gullies full of lush green laurel, gunnera, and native fuchsias, the terrain had a tropical feel. The top of the mountain ridge, from around 13,000-15,000 feet, was dominated by alder trees (*Alnus acuminate*). Like all cloud forests, the limbs and trunks of the larger trees were coated in epiphytes such as ferns, mosses, cacti, bromeliads, orchids, all entwined to make an aerial community of plants rooted not in soil but in bark, branch, and each other. On one limb a cream-backed woodpecker, a bird so big and flashy it made me think of the ivory bill, worked to excavate its hole. Flakes of mossy wood flew from the branch and made a large splattering of wood chips at the base of the tree.

From the narrow trails that wound up and down through the reserve, we finally descended to the orchards planted in the 1920s by Federico Ebber, the original Yugoslavian owner of the property. Magnolias, orange trees, pears, and cycads (plants resembling palms but not the palm or Arecaceae family) appeared and, bordering the trail, the sweet hues of pink and white domestic lilies and multicolored gladiolus welcomed us back to the hacienda.

As the last slivers of daylight faded with the taste of maté still on our tongues, Ricardo began a story about poachers. Someone was entering the reserve and gathering moss for Christmas decorations. Ricardo knew from talking with local people in the community who they might be and where they were getting in, so he took a book, sat at the back entrance on a log, and waited. He did this for several days and finally the poachers showed up. He explained to them that the moss was a vulnerable species, and that by overharvesting it, the species might disappear. The poachers nodded and left, never to return.

Ricardo's story of poaching ends happily and, in truth, there was not a lot at stake. Small holiday decorations are rather frivolous in the greater scheme of things, but poaching in some parts of the world is serious. The International Fund for Animal Welfare reports that poaching has generated over $19 billion annually and its black market economy is responsible for the support of terrorist groups (Criminal Nature 2013). It is not just an environmental problem but has grown into a serious criminal and security issue, and its devastation wrecks not only vulnerable individual species but leads to serious deterioration of entire ecosystems.

Several days before visiting Reserva de Huaico, we had explored the chaco habitats around Salta, one on a private ranch near La Lucinda and several others on private lands. The chaco is an ecosystem composed of a mosaic of arid grassland and open forest maintained by natural disturbances such as fire and/or floods. With logging, grazing, and plowing, these habitats are disappearing like the yungas at an alarming rate.

The chaco around Salta is part of a larger region known as the Gran Chaco, a massive hot semiarid plain lying east of the Andes stretching across northern Argentina, eastern Bolivia, and Paraguay, encompassing a lowland region the size of Texas. At least 1.2 million acres or roughly 10 percent of the Gran Chaco have been deforested from 2010 to 2012 for cattle ranches, according to Guyra, an environmental group in Paraguay (Romero 2012).

It was a pleasant morning but it would turn beastly hot as the day progressed. The vegetation, typical thornbush chaco, consisted of thickets of *Prosopis ruscifolia* (the most common shrubby bush), cacti (*Opuntia* species), and scraggly trees known as quebracho (*Schinopsis* species). Armadillos were out foraging and a chaco tortoise (*Chelonoidis petersi*) crawled out from under a star cactus as we made our way through the shrub. Its shell, the color of butterscotch brindled with dark brown streaks, reminded me of my guitar picks so long ago in my college days of the 1960s. How curious that a turtle shell could remind me of those times when we made folk music. I remember reading that tortoiseshell was originally harvested from hawksbill turtles and used for combs and sunglasses frames, but in the 1970s it was banned and replaced with a synthetic plastic. It seems our history so often involves making our trinkets on the backs of other creatures. If we could find ways to make the things we need (or maybe just think we need) without exploiting and irrevocably damaging our fellow species, how much wiser that would be. Certainly, those conservationists who have had the wisdom to raise such issues and suggest means to alter our behavior by finding more sustainable solutions are to be praised.

Our tour of the region would also include several national parks (Los Cardones, Laguna de los Pozuelos, and Calilegua) and a provincial park (Yala). Calilegua and Yala were short day trips to the yunga-cloud forest habitats, while Yala Provincial Park necessitated an afternoon along the Yala River where torrent ducks and rufous-throated dippers navigated the white waters. Calilegua National Park, located on the west slope of the Calilegua Mountain range, is land donated to the government by the Blackear family, owners of the sugar company, Ledesma. The land serves to protect the watershed for the sugar growing and processing industry. The sugarcane fields irrigated by the pristine waters coming from the slopes of this mountain range will remain clean as long as the land is a national park.

Los Cardones National Park, west of Salta, and Laguna de los Pozuelos, north of Salta, are habitats of the high Andes known as the altiplano, the puna, or the paramo. Mario Mosqueira, a biologist and colleague of the Clarks acted as both our guide and driver, and provided not only a steady hand on the wheel as we climbed the mountains but a wealth of information on the terrain.

The outing to Los Cardones began with strong coffee and home-made biscuits at a local truck stop in the Lerma Valley. From the town of Cachi, we crossed the Rio Cachi, stopped briefly to pick up empanadas for lunch, and began the climb up into the mountains via a series of winding switchbacks. At around 3,000 feet the desert was speckled with small patches of churqui or acacia (*Acacia caven*) and at 6,000 feet the acacia disappeared and the columnar cactus known as cardones began. The arms of these old cactuses (*Echinopsis candicans*) held bromeliads and nest holes but at 10,000 feet, they too gave way and the vegetation turned to grasses. At 15,000 feet we arrived at a pull-off over-looking the Enchanted Valley. A picture postcard of a vista, it was well named. A narrow trail took us through red rock outcrop-pings and sections of wet patches where a lily-like plant dotted the spongy ground. There were smatterings of deep green Jun-cus reeds, tiny yellow and pink alpine-like flowers, lupine, and a groundcover that resembled sensitive fern, all plants that had the diminutive look of damp alpine. The trail led to another over-look where a cattle ranch sprawled below. It belonged to a for-mer governor of the Salta providence, Mario said. It seems that the world over, our politicians manage to acquire the most beau-tiful lands.

We rested, munching empanadas on a flat rock with a cloudless blue sky as roof and the thin crisp air as dining room walls. Back to the van and driving a short way to an open prairie, we spotted an ornate tinamou moving though the roadside grasses. This ground-dwelling bird, the size of a small chicken, looks and behaves much like the more familiar U.S. prairie chicken with its foraging habits and its cryptic plumage, but it is a far rarer bird of high altitudes. Like all tinamous—its forty-seven species are all neotropical—their small wings and lack of tails make for poor flying and even poorer steering, and they regularly crash into objects when taking off and landing. How this awkward bird survives in the harsh puna where life is so sparse seemed rather remarkable.

As the late afternoon sun threw its light on the mountains, it created a scene as spectacular as the one we had seen climbing up, and we headed back to Salta in the glow of desert twilight. The next leg of the tour, Laguna de los Pozuelos National Park, required an overnight in the village of Abra Pampa. North from Jujuy through the spectacular Humahuaca Valley, we rode along a chain of mountains that could easily compete with any of the world's great scenic canyons. The mountain mural consisted of nearly every red shade in the color wheel with black and greens mixed in to form a technicolor screen softened with a gauzy scrim. The route was not only gorgeous but a historical route. The ancient cultural trek was called the Camino Real Inca route (or the Royal Road) and it allowed connection for the high Andean peoples with the temperate plains. It contained many archaeological sites and reflected a long and rich history of communication and trade. In the town of Uquia, we stopped at the tiny church of San Francisco de Padua to view the Àngeles Arcabuceros. The angels filled the church walls with glorious colors and images. Painted as Spanish aristocrats, the angels carried muzzle-loaded firearms and had wings in the shape and color of flamingos. Their puffy sleeves, fancy leggings, shoe bows, large-brimmed hats, flared coats, and cravats were flamingo pink. Rafael and Gabriel were especially stunning, wearing green brocade and framed in wreaths of pink roses. Mario explained that he thought this stop a fitting prelude to the

Laguna Pozuelos where more than 25,000 flamingos find sanctuary.

As we made our way to Abra Pampa, an occasional roadside shrine decorated with red flags appeared. Mario explained that the shrines were for Antonio Gil, a local folk hero and gaucho who, legend had it, took from the rich and gave to the poor. He was the region's Robin Hood, and small offerings of flowers and relics lay scattered around the shrines perhaps in hopes of help from the robber saint.

It wasn't only the 12,000-foot altitude with its cold thin air but the thin mattresses and thin blankets that made for a restless night. Hot coffee, fresh eggs, toast, and a bright sun the next morning soon dispelled the night's discomfort. From the high plains of Abra Pampa, the road climbed even higher into the mountains and crossed a terrain of uncommon starkness. The treeless landscape was dotted with shrubs called tola (*Parastrephia lepidophylla*) and bunchgrass (*Festuca* species). Mario pointed out green patches that were in sharp contrast to the arid rocky terrain. He called them bofedales and said they were high Andean peat bogs. The ecology of these bogs is not well understood and remains somewhat of an anomaly in the harsh landscape of the puna. Cushion plants or cojines (*Oxychloe andina, Patosia clandestine*, and several other species) make up the primary vegetation but there may be possibly new and unidentified species for some curious botanist or naturalist to come along and study.

As we crested a high point in the road and descended into the valley, the desert stretched out as a vast flat plain. While the valley had no visible signs of human habitation, Mario explained that many small villages were scattered throughout its million acres. The area around the lake is part of the Los Pozuelos National Park and National Monument, a RAMSAR site (RAMSAR sites are wetlands of international importance), and conserved as a UNESCO Biosphere Reserve.

From the parking area to the shoreline of the lake was a long walk, but the landscape was mesmerizing. Nothing grew taller than the grass, the sky was so close it felt touchable, and the mountains in pinks and mauves dappled with darker splotches of cloud shadows ringed the horizons and served as the focal point in the hypnotic, disorienting landscape. In such a thin atmosphere where light is less attenuated, everything takes on a surreal quality. Small herds of guanacos moved away and out of our direction. An Andean lapwing protecting her chicks squawked and made loud wing flapping noises to let us know she had been disturbed and to warn us to stay away from her nest. The lake was amassed with flamingos. All along the shore and far out into the water, flamingos bent their heads down into the salty lagoon waters, perfecting the art of serious feeding. We identified the three species, Andean, Chilean, and puna flamingos, and spent a leisurely few hours identifying some of the other waterfowl.

As afternoon passed, we tried to think of excuses not to leave, but realizing that driving in the dark might not be a good idea given the rough wilderness terrain and the winding road, we made our way back to Salta. As we drove back through the stunning landscape, I thought of all the places we had seen. Collectively, the preserves and parks represented not only a range of habitats and elevations, from the chaco lowlands to the cloud forest-yungas to the high puna, but all the different means by which land is protected and managed in the region. We had traveled to parks managed by the government at the national and state (or provincial) level as well as private lands owned by individuals and NGOs, and discovered that, like the diversity of habitats, many are the ways the Argentinian people are protecting their lands.

At Reserva del Huaico for a final evening of birding with the Clarks and with night erasing the last traces of sky, we hopped into Ricardo's jeep for a final twilight jaunt through the preserve. For almost an hour, we searched the trees along the road and in a small clearing for a yunga screech owl that had been calling.

Unable to spot it, we finally gave up and headed back to the house, but just as we were leaving, a scissortail nightjar flew up and over the road, and a guan as big as a turkey waddled awkwardly out into the headlights like an apparition and then disappeared like smoke into the grasses. So the day ended not with a whimper of disappointment but with a considerable bang. Back in town and our hotel in Salta, I thought how gracious the Clarks had been to share their home and evenings with us. How grateful I was to know folks like the Clarks and Mario Mosqueira, who care deeply about the natural world and live their lives trying to preserve it. If the sharing of maté could bond anyone in friendship, I could think of no better friends in the world than these dedicated conservationists.

DESERTS

CHAPTER 13.

Sky Islands and a Desert River: United States, Arizona, New Mexico, Texas

If the Chihuahua Desert were a flat tortilla covering southern Texas, New Mexico, and Arizona, the bubbles rising from its flour-colored plain would be the sky islands. The term "sky islands," first coined by the naturalist Weldon Heald (1967), refers to mountains that pushed up from the desert millions of years ago. Like all islands these mountains have distinct plants and animals and their biology/natural history has been described by a number of authors, most notably by David Quammen (2004), John McPhee (1981), Richard Shelton (1992), and Gary Nabhan (1985). My ramblings about the southwest were mostly among the sky islands of the Davis Mountains, the Guadeloupe Mountains, and the Chiricahua Mountains with a brief visit to the San Pedro Riparian Conservation Area.

Chiricahua National Monument

At the convergence of four biogeological zones, Chiricahua National Monument is a mixture of Chihuahua and Sonora desert, Rocky Mountain, and Sierra Madre habitats. A full canvas of desert and mountain species, the collage begins with ground-level plants such as agaves, prickly pear, hedgehog cactus, and yuccas and then taller shrubby juniper and piñon pines, and finally the high-canopied evergreen trees of Apache, Ponderosa, and Chihuahua pines: Arizona cypress, Douglas and white fir, Engelmann spruce, and manzanita; plus the deciduous oaks and sycamores.

We had come to this blending of ecozones to see the red-faced warbler known to breed in the area. A popular trail of the Chiricahua National Monument, Echo Canyon Trail loops three miles through Bonita Canyon and was the trail we chose as the most likely to find the warbler. I tried to keep my attention on the trail, but an incident at breakfast earlier that morning weighed heavily in my thoughts. A woman had come into the Portal cafe upset about a man she saw on the road. She was a birder as evident from her safari shirt, zip-offs, hiking boots, and binoculars. She explained that the man was weaving and stumbling about and she didn't know what to do. She had rolled down her window just enough to pass him a bottle of water—he was a fearful sight, she said, with his face peeling and bloodshot eyes—and then had driven off. The waitress said he was an illegal and they had them all the time. They came across the desert, got dehydrated, and some died. The border patrol usually picked them up and dropped them back over the border. The woman birder was clearly upset not only by the encounter, but perhaps by the casualness and sense of helplessness at the situation.

I learned this situation was not an uncommon event. Many illegal immigrants die in the desert. According to Ananda Rose, author of *Showdown in the Sonoran Desert: Religion, Law and the Immigration Controversy* (Rose 2012), over 2,000 in the past ten years have perished in the desert but few reports ever make the news. Luis Alberto Urrea's (2004) *The Devil's Highway: A True Story* tells the story of twenty-six Mexican men who tried to cross the border into the United States through the Sonora desert. Twelve died excruciating deaths in the heat; the remaining men were arrested by the border patrol and deported back to Mexico. These men were not robbers or criminals but were simply looking for a way to provide for their families.

The Echo Canyon trail began as a rather ordinary path among flat gray rocks, sloped downward, and wound through narrow beige-colored boulders. Lined with dull dry shrubs and grasses initially, the path opened after a few hundred feet into a gallery of rock sculptures. The crimson and russet rocks were tinted with yellow-green lichens against the vibrant mineral colors of weathered tuff, creating a scene as rich as any scenic rock formation in the world. The trail passed a sheer rock face and then continued through a cavern formed by an enormous boulder suspended between two columns. After a narrow tunnel, the view opened into a stunning vista. The formation, known as the Grottoes, stretched out like an army of giant stone soldiers marching down a valley of spires. The spires, called hoodoos, were as exotic as their name implied. There were towers and columns, rocks that looked like organ pipes and totem poles, boulders the size of buildings balanced on inch-long stems, steles inscribed with lichens. There were mushrooms and pinnacles and steeples, altars and stacks of saucer-shaped rocks, some rounded, some flat, some spiked. It was a stunning landscape of sculptured stone.

The only sound was the wind, a soft whistling moan. In a grove of conifers, the outline of a small bird appeared. It was a red-faced warbler perched high on a fir branch; its crimson face, neck, and breast accented in black glowed like a Christmas light bulb. The wind seemed to have conjured up the very bird we were looking for.

Not a lot is known about this warbler's conservation status, but populations may be declining. The bird breeds in the high elevation of these mountains and winters in southern Mexico and Central America. It's a foliage gleaner, eating insects from the outer branches of fir, pine, and oaks where it also makes its nest. The bird looked right at home in its deep green sanctuary.

We watched the bird for some time on the dark branch against that spectacular landscape. It was comforting to see the bird in its summer home; something about the majestic landscape as background for this tiny warbler spoke of rightness. I found myself thinking, "let us hope for a world where every creature can find sanctuary, sanctuary for the Mexican immigrant, for the red-faced warbler, and for me."

San Pedro Riparian National Conservation Area

Fifty miles southwest of the Chiricahua National Monument near Sierra Vista, Arizona, the San Pedro River is "a modern miracle, the last undammed free-flowing river in the southwest" (Shelton 1992: 142). Originating around Sonora, Mexico, the river flows north one hundred and forty miles to join the Gila River near Winkelman, Arizona. One hundred and fifty years ago before extensive human settlement, the river was a system of vast marshes known as cienegas, wetlands in the heart of a desert. Removal of the beaver and the vegetation that maintained the wetlands, plus increased land use, caused the river to channelize and the wetlands to disappear. Without the dams and irrigation forces that turned many of the rivers of the southwest into dry gullies, the San Pedro still runs wide and strong through the Chihuahua and Sonora deserts.

We were on the San Pedro Trail in the San Pedro Riparian Conservation Area, a forty-mile stretch of over 57,000 acres along the river, in search of the elegant trogon. Through portions of uplands with creosote, acacia, and tarbush and then down along the riverbanks with tall cottonwood, willows, and sycamore, we meandered looking for this tropical bird. The elegant trogon is a passerine that winters in southern Mexico and Central America; its northernmost breeding grounds are in the area. Like an owl, the trogon can see in low light and can turn its head nearly 360 degrees. The male has a deep metallic green head, black face and throat, a white collar, and a red-orange breast. This flycatcher can remain perched upright on a branch for hours, and its long lovely tail, copper-green on the upper side with a black tip, drops down like an elegant wall hanging. Its white underbelly has fine horizontal black barrings. A tropical bird uncommon for the United States, it is one of the southwestern birds well worth seeing and many birders come to the area for its sightings.

What makes the river and the conservation area remarkable is that it took an act of congress to create it. To get Congress to agree on anything these days is noteworthy, so Richard Shelton's calling it a miracle has several elements of truth. In the early 1970s hundreds of people from many environmental groups ranging from the Sierra Club and the Nature Conservancy, to the Bureau of Land Management came together to support leg-islation to protect the river and create the conservation area. For over fifteen years, environmentalists worked diligently until the Arizona Congressional delegation and the U.S. Congress in 1988 finally enacted legislation creating it. Today the Friends of the San Pedro River, with its hundreds of volunteer members keeps watch over the river (Shelton 1992). It is one of the best examples of successful local, regional, and national collaborative efforts to protect the disappearing riparian desert habitat of the Southwest.

Though we spent the morning searching for a trogon, we never located one, but we did see the yellow-billed cuckoo and Bell's vireo, and left not with disappointment but with a sense of com-fort knowing the conservation area is home to over one hundred species of breeding birds, 250 species of migrants, and many wintering birds of conservation concern, not to mention the hundreds of plants and animals unique to the desert riparian ecosystem.

Guadeloupe Mountains and Carlsbad Caverns

The dingy motel we stayed in overnight and the lukewarm tea the next morning were not the best experience, but the crisp morning air had an invigorating quality. The sun was still below the horizon and the stars blinked brightly as only they can in the cold dry New Mexico desert air. We drove from the motel to the caverns along the dark highway with the car's headlights a narrow cone illuminating not much more than the centerline. The turnoff and parking area were really dark, but along the walkway to the cave there was just enough light to move safely to the concrete seats that encircled the cave entrance.

Carlsbad Caverns is the largest cave system in North America with over one hundred known caves, and an estimated 300 yet to be explored. A cowboy named Jim White discovered the caverns at the turn of the last century and he traversed them with simple ropes and ladders. In 1930 its 47,000 acres was declared a national park. We had walked through the caverns the day before and marveled at its stone gardens. As we descended into the damp cold limestone, stalagmites and stalactites glistened with watery minerals. The cave's formation is an epic story of the transporting of stone, where millions of years of water have dissolved calcite in one place and deposited it in another, creating rooms and halls of sculptures. Called speleothems, the rock formations fashioned an infinite variety of shapes, from pearls to petals, from draperies to veiled statues, wedding cakes to soda straws, needles to toothpicks, fingers to troll faces, pagodas to shrines. Every surface had the luscious texture of desserts, the shine of chocolate pudding, tapioca, buttered pecan ice cream, lemon icing. And among the formations, pools of water lay still as mirrors.

As we waited for the bats in the dusky dawn on the cold concrete seats, ten minutes passed, then fifteen and twenty. I shivered and bunched my hands deep into my coat pockets. Just above the mouth of the cave at the skyline, a few dark squiggly lines appeared like eye-floaters that come on when one's blood pressure rises. Black tildes began appearing and seemed to drop into the mouth of the cave as a soft buzzing sound began. Then more appeared, clusters of a few, then dozens, and then hundreds as they zoomed down into the cave like thrown darts. More and more filled the air in free fall. Bats materialized from the dusky sky and plummeted into the cave like dropped pebbles. For over two hours Mexican free-tail bats gorged and, finally, full of moths and insects from the night's feasting, returned home to their cave.

Mexican free-tail bats are one of the most widespread species of mammals in North America, and their habitat ranges from the southern United States throughout Mexico, Central America, and South America. Most are migratory. The Carlsbad bats, inhabiting these caves from April to October, winter in Mexico. Once there were nearly nine million Carlsbad bats, but their numbers have declined to about 800,000 because of pesticides such as DDT (banned in the United States since 1972 but still widely used in Mexico) and dieldrin, and the boring of a shaft through the ceiling of the main roosting area of the cave to provide access for guano mining. The alteration caused the temperature, humidity, and airflow to change in the roosting area and resulted in massive bat die-offs.

When the last of the bats were back, snuggled deep in their corners hanging by their toes, wrapped in the cocoon of their capes, the sun was up and the sky was a pale milky rose. We walked back to our car along with the other spectators who had come to see the bats. An elderly couple walked along beside us. He had on a green baseball cap with a John Deere logo and she was in a floral print dress with a heavy pink sweater. They held hands. He nodded, smiled, and said, "We've been coming here for fifty years to see the bats."

I marveled at the statistics that claimed over a million visitors come each year to this place. Certainly the spectacular cave was a draw but I was happy to know that most people come to see the bats. In this world where one in every five mammals is at risk of extinction, and where most people have to go to zoos to see wild animals, it was good to know there are folks who need to see the bats at home in their natural cave sanctuary.

Davis Mountains State Park

The woman in the big SUV pulled into the lodge's parking lot next to us, hopped out, and began unpacking. She said, "We usually come here for the annual observatory party; we love having a few drinks and watching the stars, but this time we're here just to get away."

We had driven from Big Bend National Park and along Skyline Drive, a seventy-mile loop through the Davis Mountains. The highway was speckled with ponderosa and piñon pines, alligator and piñon juniper, emory and gray oaks, and then passed through a grassland valley where horned larks and western meadowlarks perched on the fence wires like clothespins. We were ready to settle in for the evening at the park lodge when we decided that after all that driving a walk around the park would be a good way to get the kinks out. With the slim hopes of glimpsing a Mexican spotted owl, we put on our binoculars and off we trekked to explore one of the trails.

The trail we chose passed an observation area where curved-billed thrashers poked and prodded, throwing up litter in their search for insects. The bird's dull gray-brown plumage interrupted by faint spots on its chest seemed rather lackluster but its eyes were target bright orange and its bill an unusual downward curve.

The scrub vegetation, mesquite, cholla cactus, little-leaf leadtree, evergreen and fragrant sumac, ocotillo and catclaw acacia crackled softly in the dry evening breeze. The smell of cooking fires drifted from the campgrounds and reminded us that we had had little to eat all day and needed to get back to the dining room before closing time. It was getting dark and the trail was getting harder to see.

A sudden rustling in the scrub brought us up short. A faint skunkish odor arose and out trotted seven javelinas, three big ones and four little ones. They crossed the trail giving us a wide berth, and with a passing glance, veered off into the underbrush. With delicate hind feet, fleshy snouts, bristly salt and pepper coats and thick manes, and a light-colored band encircling their necks, collared peccaries have to be one of the most unsightly mammals of the desert.

But peccaries have gotten a bum rap. Perhaps for the same reasons that some people dislike other races and ethnicities, the aversion to peccaries comes from attitudes often based on misinformation. While reports of dog killings by peccaries in the suburbs of Tucson and Phoenix are probably not exaggerated, they belie the fact that any creature when cornered by a barking dog might aggressively fight back. Claims that peccaries carry disease such as pseudorabies or swine flu, which affect livestock, are unsubstantiated, and it is well-known that humans carry far more diseases than these ungulates. In Arizona, peccaries, or javelinas as they are called, are considered "big game" and prized as great trophies. Organized hunts with dogs, seasons based on weapons such as muzzle-loaders, handguns, and bows, and special packaged deals of three-day hunts for $1,600/person are offered. Apparently to kill one suggests an act of great skill and courage. In a nation where we are not protein deprived and where hunting is entertainment and sport, the interest in acquiring a photograph or the stuffed head of a creature, killed and posed with teeth bared, suggests a level of brutality that reeks of ancient atavistic coliseum-going.

Peccaries are actually not desert animals; they evolved in the rain forests of South America and migrated north. Their territory now includes much of the Sonora and Chihuahua deserts. Fortunate to have migrated at a time when there were no borders, I suppose it might be said, they are not an invasive species (nor illegal aliens) but are now considered part of the natural desert fauna. In Davis Mountain State Park, peccaries are hunted only once a year in January in a public bow hunt. Otherwise, they are allowed to live out their lives in relative peace. As we made our way back to the lodge and dinner, I thought, perhaps such limited sanctuary (being hunted only once a year) for some species in a land where borders are so strictly enforced and illegal aliens are treated so poorly is the best one can hope for.

CHAPTER 14.

Where the Desert Meets the Sea: Mexico, The Baja

"There is no "I" in team!" Denver exclaimed over the music of the mariachi band that marched onto the balcony and began serenading us. Around the table at Dirty Sanchez we were getting acquainted with our fellow travelers: Denver and Megan, our guides, Judy and Darla, our fellow birders. It would prove to be a very congenial team with no overbearing "I's" and lots of good companionship, always the best way to travel, with folks who engage in life with a sense of joy and humor. Denver explained our route would be to leave Los Cabos, drive from the southern tip of the Baja peninsula north to La Paz, spend some days on the Sea of Cortez, cross the peninsula to Puerto San Carlos on Magdalena Bay for some whale watching, and return to Los Cabos.

The afternoon we arrived in Los Cabos was a relief from the New York winter. Having seen the Pacific Ocean from the high cliffs of northern California, fringed by massive trees in Oregon, and speckled with sea stacks in Washington, I remember its oceanic shore as majestic, but here it seemed more familiar, more homey, more like the Gulf Coast with gently sloping sandy beaches and soft mellow waves. We sat beneath a big red umbrella eating chicken enchiladas and drinking iced tea with '60s tunes playing in the background. Songs like "He's a Rebel,"

"Johnny Angel," "Let's Dance," and "Breaking Up Is Hard to Do" played nostalgic, and with the bright sun and blue waters lifting away the hours of crowded airports and jarring flights, the New York winter began to dissolve. We took off our shoes and walked the pebbled beach letting the waves nibble our feet. For over twenty miles from Cabo San Lucas to San Jose del Cabo, the shoreline was lined with hotels and condos. As an environmentalist, it might be easy for me to bemoan such development, but as I walked the warm pebbles I understood why people come here and why inevitably the water's edge becomes developed. Our desire for comfort and beauty drives a process that is unlikely to end. Perhaps the best we can hope for is that shorelines develop in the most sustainable ways possible.

Before we left Los Cabos to begin our journey to La Paz, we visited a tidal creek in a protected area known as Estero de San Jose del Cabo State Reserve. At the entrance to the trail in this small wetlands among the condos and development, a flock of white-collared seedeaters fluttered up from palm fronds and flew off over the creek. A great egret still as a lawn statue ignored us and continued its meditative one-legged stance beneath bell-bottomed cypress trees. In an open field bordered with scrub, a verdin was catching insects. Returning to its perch over and over again, its yellow head above rufous shoulders made a bright splatter on the fence.

The small town of El Triunfo on the way to La Paz was a step back into the boom times of the 1860s when gold and silver were mined. Once the largest city and cultural center of the Baja, it was now a sleepy town of only several hundred people. When the mines played out in the 1920s, the town dwindled to crumbling brick walls, abandoned bulk works, smelter pits, and two smelter stacks. White lettering on the side of one of the old brick chimneys read "1890"; the other, shorter square chimney, had been designed by Gustave Eiffel of Eiffel Tower fame. I wondered if the music of the world-renowned pianist of the times, Francisca

Mendoza, who lived, taught, and performed in this town, ever drifted like phantom notes on the warm afternoon breeze.

A dry gulch provided thicket birds, orange-crowned warblers, and blue-gray gnatcatchers. As the afternoon heat grew heavier, we walked slowly among the leafless branches of creosote, mesquite, bursage, and low shrubs. On our way back to the van, an old couple stood on the roadside. The woman's black knee-high stockings had so many runs they looked like a road map, and her tiny stick legs seemed barely able to support her. She moved in a stiff arthritic manner. He, too, could hardly move, and his coat and trousers were so dusty that when he did move, a cloud rose from him. His hands were gnarled and the color of old pine knots. They looked so poor and malnourished I felt guilty eating a power bar. They seemed to embody the place, the old and infirm against the background of a once-thriving, now dis-integrating town.

On to La Paz, we turned off the Baja Highway into the city. The road ran along the Sea of Cortez, and the slow-moving traffic allowed us a look at the hotels, restaurants, and shops. People walking, running, and skating on the seaside gave the place a festive feel. The water was deep blue and the clouds looked like spun sugar. Denver pointed out the Hotel Paradise where John Steinbeck and Ed Ricketts stayed during their expe-dition of the Sea of Cortez. In 1939 Steinbeck and Ricketts, a biologist, chartered a trawler called the *Western Flyer* and spent six weeks observing and collecting along the shores of the Sea of Cortez. The narrative of their expedition, *Sea of Cortez: A Leisurely Journal of Travel and Research* (Steinbeck and Ricketts 1941), describes the many wonders of the region's ecology. Stein-beck writes, "It seems apparent that species are only commas in a sentence, that each species is at once the point and the base of a pyramid...One [species] merges in another, groups melt into eco-logical groups..." Steinbeck was probably far ahead of his times regarding the interconnections of life. "It is not clear whether

Steinbeck's thinking influenced Aldo Leopold, Rachel Carson, and those other naturalists, scientists, and philosophers who formulated the new prevailing environmental dogma, but the we-are-all-in-this-together theme was a distinct one…[it] included everything from sea slugs to the stars, anticipated ideas about the web of life, the rights of rocks and other tenets of current holistic ecology" (Gilbert 2001).

The first morning in La Paz we rose early and made our way to the tidal flats west of the city. A dozen magnificent frigate birds soared in wide lazy spirals, tails opening in sharp "Vs," and above the dense thickets of the tidal mangroves, brown pelicans cruised the sky in dotted chevrons. The early morning sun, which gives everything a softer look, didn't improve the appearance of the mangroves. Mangroves have little appeal to the average person. Their dirty tangled branches catch the trash of the sea and everything from plastic bags to food wrappers was caught up in them. Even Steinbeck and Ricketts had few pleasant things to say about mangroves, claiming their roots "gave off clicking sounds and (their) odor was disgusting." But these ugly bushes are undeniably important in the ecology of coastlands. They are the forests of the sea's edge: they stabilize the shoreline, provide nursery grounds for many estuarine organisms, and are the source of the enormous biological productivity of the coastal ecosystem. They fix more carbon worldwide than rain forests. Estimates suggest that one-third of the mangroves of the world have been cleared for housing development and resorts, and they are disappearing faster than the rain forests. While efforts are being made to save them by such biologists as Candy Feller (2007) and Kennedy Warne (2011), mangrove forests may become a thing of the past.

From a branch near the top of the mangroves, Denver heard the call of the mangrove warbler. A subspecies of the yellow warbler, the mangrove warbler has a variation of the yellow warbler's song: "sweet, sweet, I'm so sweet." The male was perched on an open branch, his rust-colored head glowing in the sun like polished mahogany. We watched for a while until the pair flew off and disappeared into another nearby tangle of mangrove branches.

With the receding tide we ventured out onto the mud flats to get a closer look at the shorebirds feeding in the shallows, but as we moved away from the shore the ground became less and less solid. When the clumps of grass gave out, the ground turned the consistency of oatmeal. Each step became a trap as we sank up to our ankles, then our calves, then almost to our knees. The mud seemed to be pulling us down, and every effort to get our feet up and out and take another step forward resulted in gurgling sucking noises. Mud splattered everywhere. I was afraid we would be up to our necks by the time we reached the low tide water's edge, but a quick decision by our guides allowed us to turn around and retreat to more stable ground. Back on solid ground and off the mud flats, we looked like chocolate Easter bunnies from the waist down.

That evening at an outdoor neighborhood restaurant called Rancho Viego everyone settled in and ordered drinks. An elderly gentleman in a suit and tie played a classical guitar for a young couple at the next table while the rising full moon cast silver shadows over everyone. After a few rounds of margaritas, the conversation turned to the birds we had seen that day. When Darla referred to "mango wobblers," everyone roared with laughter. The resulting wisecracks ranged from, "Is that your impression of Elmer Fudd?" to "It's the Spanish 'r' that is so difficult," to "Is a wobbler like a gobbler?" and a number of other progressively sillier comments that I have since forgotten, probably the influence of the margaritas. While the details of our conversation might be blurred in my memory, the warmth of the evening, the laughter, the moonlight, the music, and the feeling of fellowship and connection with my companions remain as vivid now as ever. That day on the mud flats and the evening dinner have remained forever entwined as part of my memories of friends and mangrove warblers.

Birding around La Paz was a hot affair. Several sites north and south of the city offered trails in a habitat considered a mixed biome where Sonora desert merges with thorn scrub habitat. The second evening after a long hot day of birding, we watched the sun sink into the Sea of Cortez north of the city at a small palapa on Balandra Beach where Ramón and his wife served us grilled garlic shrimp and bottles of cold Negro Modelo. Below the coral sky, the slouching of the incoming tide and the piercing cries of the gulls provided beach music. The air had the soft tinge of a summer evening as folks began to pick up their towels and sandals and walk back to their cars, leaving the beach to the gulls. Someone turned on a radio that played a melancholy Spanish love song as night lowered her curtain.

The music fit this balmy beach that was once the target of developers but had been saved by the efforts of the local citizenry. Through the action of local residents, several civil groups, and environmentalists, Colectivo Balandra was formed, a petition was written asking that the area be protected, and in 2008 state officials designated the beach a Natural Protected Area (White 2008). In 2012, it was named a Federal Area of Flora and Fauna Protection (Jauregui 2013).

Offshore the island known as Isla Espiritu Santos (a UNESCO Biosphere and World Heritage Site) became a dark hump as the sun sank and the mound disappeared into the night sky. In 2005, this uninhabited island, one in the chain of 244 islands in the Sea of Cortez, was purchased with funding from the Nature Conservancy, World Wildlife Fund, and Conservation International and turned over to the Mexican Park Service. Twenty miles long, thirty-one square miles of black lava and pink volcanic ash, the island has a limited flora and fauna, but several invasive species eradication programs removed the rats, cats, and goats to keep the island's five endemic species of mice and one snake in balance. A no-catch zone surrounds the island, but visitors can kayak and swim with the resident sea lions.

As night descended and it was time to go, we said goodnight to Balandra Beach and Espiritu Island. It lifted my spirits to witness these protected lands and to know all the many ways our Mexican neighbors organize to protect and keep their coastal lands natural and pristine.

From the east coast of the Baja and the Sea of Cortez to the west coast and Puerto San Carlos, the highway through the plain of Magdalena offered an exotic landscape. Plants such as the big-arm raised cactuses known as cardons (*Pachycereus pringlei*), giant agaves (*Agave* species), and yuccas (*Yucca datilillo*) gave the desert an alien look, but it was the boojum tree (*Fouquieria columnaris*), resembling a thin upside-down carrot covered with spiny twigs, and the creeping devil cactus (*Stenocereus eruca*) crawling over the fields like fuzzy octopuses that created a truly alien feel. Joseph Krutch called the boojum tree "a freak in the vegetable world" (Krutch 1986: 81) and one so queer "only a botanist could love" (Krutch 1986: 72). This southern part of the Sonora desert was certainly a more bizarre and wilder place than its tamer cousin to the north.

We arrived in Puerto San Carlos after dark, dined at a nearby restaurant where three matronly ladies served us grilled grouper and cold beer, and turned in early for the next morning's pre-dawn wake-up call. Denver had hired a panga (the small blue boat of the region) and driver to take us out into the Bay of Magdalena to see the gray whales.

Hot coffee, a quick breakfast, and the day began. The morning was grand! The rising sun sparkled off the waves and the sea mirrored the cloudless sky. Our driver explained that about 200 whales lived in the shallow bay this time of year. The males in deeper waters would breach and flip their tails in spectacular splashy displays. Each whale had unique markings of encrusted barnacles, parasites, and scars etching its many watery years—they live as long as we do, around seventy years. The females with their babies in the shallower waters were quieter. To spot them we watched for blows. A column of water would lift thirty feet in the air with a loud gush of spray, and stalks of white foam would rise from a hump and break into rainbows. It was as if the sea was sprouting rainbows. When our driver maneuvered the boat up to a mother and her calf, I reached out and touched the back of the baby whale. It felt like a wet sponge. The mother and calf rolled and glided together in a fluidity that seemed to have the quality of a dream, and for a moment I wondered if I was only dreaming.

Gray whales are among the oldest mammals on earth, having been around for 30 million years. Hunted almost to extinction in the 1800s and early 1900s, they disappeared from the Atlantic Ocean but two small populations, one along the North American Pacific coast and the other along the Japanese coast, have survived. In the 1940s, with only a few hundred gray whales remaining, an international agreement was enacted to protect them and today there are about 20,000. The whales travel over 5,000 miles from Alaskan waters to the Baja where the shallow lagoon protects the babies from sharks and orcas. As baleen whales, they filter food from the rich hypersaline waters of Magdalena Bay and thrive, protected until they migrate back up to Alaskan waters.

After the whales, everything else seemed anti-climactic, but our time in the Baja was nearing an end, and it was time to return to Los Cabos and catch our flight home. On the way back, the small artisan village of Todos Santos provided lunch at the Hotel California and a stop at the Sierra de la Laguna Biosphere Reserve. The turnoff to the reserve was an inconspicuous dirt road running through miles of thorn shrub. The reserve is a dry tropical forest ecosystem with habitats that change with elevation. At the lower elevations the habitat is typical Sonora Desert and at the higher elevation, in the Sierra Laguna Mountains, pine-oak forest with species such as the evergreen oak (*Quercus devia*) and the Mexican piñon (*Pinus cembroides* subsp. *lagunae*) dominate. We explored some of the trails at the lower elevation for several hours, and as we were about to leave, Denver spotted a cape pigmy owl. As president and founder of the Owl Research Institute (ORI, see website), an educational/conservation NGO in Charlo, Montana, he has been active in owl research and conservation for over thirty years. And Denver knows owls. The owl, endemic to the Baja, is also called the Baja pigmy owl, and as we watched the tiny bird, it seemed the perfect finale to our visit. The owl was a reaffirmation that on this peninsula of desert and sea, where so much development has occurred in the past 40 years, it is also the place of many sites protected by the efforts of conservationists.

CHAPTER 15.

African Safari: Africa, Namibia, Botswana, Zambia

I might have left Windhoek, the capital of Namibia, thinking it was a prosperous city, as the hotel where we met our group was located in an area that resembled an upscale Phoenix neighborhood. If we had not driven out of the city and seen the squatter settlements, I would have thought Windhoek to be an affluent city in an affluent country. But the thousands of tiny huts constructed of sheet metal, wood scraps, and throwaways stretching out over the highlands spoke of a different reality. There was no evidence of electricity, power lines, proper sanitation, telephones, grocery stores, or any of the amenities associated with civilization, just miles and miles of shanties covering the hillsides. As in so many cities of the world, the poor seem to be part of a target either as a concentric ring surrounding a city or forming its center core.

From Windhoek, we traveled north skirting the great southern African deserts, the Kalahari to the east and the Namib to the west. It was the beginning of the rainy season and the landscape, a habitat known as the bush veldt or thorn shrub veldt, was mint green. The trees consisted primarily of acacia (*Acacia* species), over fifty species, the most common ones being the camel thorn tree, buffalo thorn tree, yellow bark acacia, and black hook acacia, which is actually an invasive from the southeastern United States.

Our first stop, a 27,000-acre private game park and lodge near Omaruru called Epako. The lodge overlooked a waterhole where giraffe, endangered white and black rhinos, eland, and kudus came to drink. With gray go-away-birds perched in the branches and on the porch railing, simply lounging on the veranda provided hours of entertainment. In the turaco family and closely related to the cuckoos, go-away-birds look like large blue jays with uniformly gray coloring and tall crests that rise when the bird is agitated. They hang around houses and farms on the lookout for handouts and can be a nuisance, likely eliciting the shout, "go away, bird!" Their alarm cry also sounds a bit like "go away!"

The evening drive to the top of a high plateau turned into a wapatuli party as we watched the sun slide below the rolling hills. The spiked fruit punch provided by the lodge was enough to get everyone a little more relaxed, and as the sky turned the color of ripe peaches and then dark plums, the feeling of camaraderie among my fellow travelers seemed to forecast a fun adventure. The landscape from our high tor was a palette of celery green hills slowly darkening to eggplant as a herd of elephants moved slowly through the bush and disappeared with the setting sun. Our driver-guide referred to the land as Damaraland, but unlike the beauty of the landscape now, its history spoke of a different story. Damaraland is an old apartheid name for southern Kaokoland, a place where the Damara people were relocated as the result of the Odendaal Plan of the 1960s. The Odendaal Plan, part of the systematic legislation to enforce racial segregation in South Africa, involved four groups—native, white, colored, and Asian. Each was separated by forced removal and representation for all but whites abolished. After the practice of apartheid ended in the 1990s, the region became known as Erongo. But some of the old names remained, and I was reminded that even though Namibia had only won its independence from South Africa in

1990, the politics of South Africa was a legacy still visible in the language of the Namibian landscape.

After the sun dipped below the horizon and the empty canisters of punch were packed up, we set out on a mission to find night-jars. With a little help from the punch, riding the dark roads looking for those cryptic night birds turned into a wild quest. Bumping along the rough terrain, stopping and jumping out of the jeep at every possible hint of nightjars, we rode until exhaustion and probably the sobering-up effect drove us back to the lodge and our beds.

The next day began with a morning drive through the bush where a couple of jackals with pups lounged in a clearing. They moved quickly back into the underbrush near a butter tree. The butter tree (*Cyphostemma currorii*), also called the cobas tree, provided a sharp contrast to the surrounding shrubby thorn trees. With its large succulent frond-like leaves, swollen trunk, and patches of peeling yellow bark, the butter tree looked more like a rain forest species. The plant's lush foliage might seem attractive to an herbivore but because it is rich in oxalic acid, especially its fruit, it is actually shunned by browsers. The toxic oxalic acid precipitates calcium and damages the kidneys of any creature that eats it.

At an ancient rock outcropping near a dry riverbed, our local guide pointed out San paintings engraved on the rocks. He explained that the ancient pictographs were thousands of years old; they depicted stick hunters with bows, elephants, giraffes, eland and other animals. The San, known as the Khoisan peoples, or the bushman, were the aborigines of southern Africa dating back 35,000 years and perhaps once numbering a quarter of a million. Today there are only about 50,000 San people left as they have been driven to near extermination by the Bantu people and white settlers. They have made their last refuge in the hostile Kalahari Desert.

An afternoon thunderstorm was the most electrifying event of the day. Resting after lunch, I noticed the sky turning darker and flashes of lightning brightening the sky. A soft far-off rumbling of thunder grew louder and louder until it burst forth like a sonic boom rattling the sliding glass doors of my room and shaking the lamps off the tables. Rain came down in torrents. The rain and thunder drowned out all other sounds. From the porch I watched the dry riverbed below the lodge fill until a river formed. Within minutes a small trickle became a stream, then a creek, then a torrential river carrying huge branches along on its raging waters. The plain became a river of red mud as the waters swept through. Then just as quickly the rain ended, the waters subsided, and a slow meandering stream pushed its way south to the Omaruru River with a cool breeze rising off its waters.

From Epako we traveled northwest to Waterberg Plateau National Park, an old German outpost that has been converted into a lodge and national park. Namibia was a German protectorate in the 1880s and a German colony until World War I, so the country has remnants of that colonial past. The sturdy red rock lodge, the squat rock cabins, the sausage on the lunch menu all evoked a distinct German flavor. The park was established in 1972 as a sanctuary for rare and endangered animals such as the black and white rhinos, sable antelope, blue wildebeest, and Cape vulture. Of the 3, 610 black rhinos remaining in the world, nearly half live on the Waterberg Plateau.

The red sandstone butte rising 1,200 feet above the savannah revealed a very different habitat from that of the thornbush. The ancient plateau, which is about twelve-and-a-half miles wide and thirty-one miles long, supports broadleaf trees such as the Kalahari apple leaf, the silver-cluster leaf, and wild syringe, giving the landscape a lusher appearance than the lacy thin-leafed acacias of the veldt. Springs at the base of the plateau ensure there is water even in the dry season, giving the park its name. Weeping wattle and lichens (over 140 different species according to the park guidebook) wallpapered the red cliffs a multitude of greens. Because of the sheer rock walls only a few trails led up to the mesa, making it a difficult place to access. Inaccessibility is frequently a key characteristic in the making of a good sanctuary.

When we returned to our cabins we interrupted a troop of baboons barging through like a gang of hoodlums knocking over trash cans and rummaging for possible morsels. We had been warned to lock our cabin doors for just that reason. Following the baboons a pack of banded mongoose came bouncing through and all I could think of was rodeo clowns. They scampered from one cabin to the next, hopping and jumping over each other, and disappeared into the underbrush just as quickly as they had come. Later that evening, we encountered another primate cousin in addition to the baboons. By the light of a full moon with an insect choir humming a little night music (did I hear someone say, "humbug"?), we discovered lesser bush babies high in the branches of the camel thorn trees. These smallest of the primates, known as galagos, are nocturnal and about the size of a squirrel. They move so agilely and quickly using their long tails as balance that it was difficult to get even a glimpse. They leaped and scurried from branch to branch but occasionally, when the headlights hit one, their big round eyes reflecting like saucers looked down at us as if in total astonishment. I thought, how different we primates are, rowdy baboons, shy bush babies, and the ever-so-curious humans. To the sound of nightjars calling in the distance, we oh-so-inquisitive primates returned to our cabins and a welcome night's rest.

The morning we left Waterberg was a misty drizzle. We all held our breath until we reached the main highway because the park road was like pudding. The rain had turned the dirt road into a mudslide and we slid and swerved until finally with a sigh of relief that we would not get stuck, we hit solid pavement. From Waterberg we traveled on to Etosha National Park, probably the best-known park in Namibia. Our plan was to stay at three different sites inside the park, at Okaukago and Haleli lodges, and in the private lodge, Mushara, just on the outskirts. Each morning and afternoon, we would drive into the park to see what was about.

The goal the first morning was to check out the seven lark species of the grasslands, and it turned out that several lions were meandering around among the larks. Two handsome young males sauntered from a grove of leadwood trees and crossed the road directly in front of the van giving us a close-up. The larks were soon forgotten in the lion sighting. But the most exciting sight of the morning was the blue crane. No one else seemed particularly excited but I was thrilled. About half a dozen clustered together in a small group and they strolled about on their long legs feeding on seeds and insects. In gray-blue coats, they moved among the grasses with the grace of a tai chi master, slowly, carefully, aware. I was suddenly transported to a time in the 1980s when I saw Rudolf Nureyev perform a ballet from, was it *Swan Lake*? Their feathers were the same color as his costume, in fact, the entire set was that color; the birds' strides, their every movement, were as graceful as his. I was awestruck.

Of the fifteen species of cranes, seven are endangered and many of the others species are categorized as vulnerable or threatened. Only about 26,000 blue cranes remain in the world. While everyone had a good look and took pictures, no one seemed as particularly impressed as I. For me, their presence was almost magical. They seem to evoke the most intense sense of refinement and elegance.

Back at the lodge, we made a brief stop for lunch, followed by a walk to the waterhole. Our guide pointed out young moringa trees (*Moringa stenopetala*) recently planted among the red bush willows along the pathways. Sadly, some tourist(s) had carved their initials on the trees' smooth silvery trunks. Moringa trees—there are thirteen species in the genus—play a significant role in the ecology of the desert because much of the plant is edible. Its high protein and vitamin content, its seeds used in traditional medicines and its leaves, for tea, make it a valuable species in harsh, dry habitats. Because of those qualities, it has been heavily exploited and is now designated a protected species.

Unlike the moringa trees, mopane trees (*Colophospermum mopae*) are abundant and they grew all over the lodge grounds. They make up about 80 percent of Etosha's trees. In the lodge's parking areas, a group of mopanes offered a large shady canopy and a place for morning birding. In the crotch of one old tree near the dining room, a pigmy owl gathered a ring of curious onlookers until the smell of frying bacon drew the crowd on into the dining tables. After breakfast a short walk around the grounds helped get the day off to a pleasant start. As the sky lightened, the sun's rays hit the leaves of the mopane trees, which are shaped like butterfly wings. It was not difficult to imagine the leaves suddenly deciding to take flight like a million green butterflies lifting off into the air leaving the tree limbs bare. There seems a touch of magic about mopane trees.

The stylish lodge, Mushara, just outside the park was our next accommodation and its decor was something out of an art magazine. The high-beamed, open-air lounge was done in African safari motif, white couches and chairs accented with zebra-striped cushions, white wicker stools, wicker chairs, plant stands and table lamps in wicker, coffee tables of polished mahogany, and long slender floor lamps resembling the horns of impalas. The chalets had thatched roofs and the beds looked fit for a palace. We were there only one night so as not to get too used to such extravagant living. The grounds had a crystal blue swimming pool surrounded by purple-pod terminalia trees in full bloom. When the breeze blew the clusters of maroon blossoms, it was easy to imagine the ruffles of square dancing skirts.

The last morning in Etosha began with a quick drive through

several of the habitats we had missed earlier. Etosha is mostly grassland savannahs with some woodlands. We had previously explored the grasslands so we made a short trip through one of the saltpans and bottomlands. We added a few more species of flamingos, hornbills and kori bustards to our sighting list, and then headed back to the main road where we caught the highway to the Caprivi Strip. Nearing what is known as the Red Line—the quarantine line used to control the spread of foot and mouth disease—we began to lose some of the touristy African safari sights and get glimpses of another Africa. Settlements of small thatch-roofed huts, often with bright red communal toilets, were the homes of subsistence farmers. These villagers grew small fields of corn and millet and had vegetable gardens enclosed with wooden pole fences.

These villages are part of one of Namibia's sixty-four community-based conservancies, which make up about 17 percent of the country's land. These areas are not parks, because people live and make their livelihood there, but they represent Namibia's concept of conservation-requires-community model. Lead by the native born conservationist, John Kaeaona, assistant director of Integrated Rural Development and Nature Conservation, he has been lauded as turning poachers into protectors and caretakers. These communities have set aside a portion of their land exclusively for wildlife and its protection. By establishing strong bonds of cooperation between local communities and wildlife protection, Namibia's conservation efforts are world renowned.

Through the city of Rundu, turning eastward along the Okavango River, we arrived at the Nkwazi Lodge in early afternoon. Our guide arranged an evening boat ride, so we all piled onto a big flat-bottomed boat that was really not much more than a raft with a motor on the back end, and we set off to explore the birds of the Okavango. After motoring upstream for a bit and spotting several species of kingfishers, egrets, and herons, we asked if we might step foot on the other shore and add Angola to our list of visited countries. The driver was amendable so we landed and everyone gingerly stepped off the boat onto the shore of a new country. Someone had a pen and a piece of cardboard on which we wrote "Illegal aliens" and group pictures were taken to document our illegal entry into Angola. Just as we were about to get back on the boat, a marsh owl flew overhead, and then another and another, until a dozen marsh owls buzzed around our heads. They were alarmed by our presence, for as benign as was our intention, our landing had created a disturbance. We left as quickly as possible so as not to disturb the owls any more than necessary. Drifting back to the lodge on the river current, we made a final stop to see a rare white-backed night heron tucked in the dense willows along the riverbanks.

The second lodge along the Okavango River, Nunda River Lodge, had lush flower gardens and cabins located right on the banks of the river. Hippos grunted late into the night as they came in and out of the river and grazed on the grassy lawns. The second night after dinner on our way back to our cabin in the dark, with the help of a lodge guard who had a headlight, we nearly ran into two hippos munching on the lawn. The guard told us as we waited for the animals to move off that more deaths were caused by encounters with hippos than with any other animal. Our near collision was enough to keep me awake for hours, but the croaking of frogs late into the night was soothing. Their cries sounded like someone calling "Maxine, Maxine, Maxine" and I drifted off to sleep to their calling.

Several visits to the "off the beaten track" Mahango Game Reserve were rewarded with a troop of vervet monkeys, roan antelope, impala, kudu, warthogs, bushbuck, and a small herd of tesessebe, all the sightings a small, well-managed African sanctuary might offer. The three habitats, grassland with acacia and bush willow borders; riverine with reed, grasses and wetland vegetation; and woodlands with patches of teak offered one of Namibia's most varied conservation areas. Of particular interest were the baobab trees (*Adansonia digitata*) that grew abundantly throughout the reserve. A grove of ancient baobabs, each tree over a thousand years old, was especially inviting. We walked around the trees, patted the old trunks, took pictures, and marveled at their enormous size. The hand-shaped leaves, which give the species its name, "digit," were dense green at the end of this rainy season. Many myths and legends revolve around these trees, often involving the tree being home to spirits. A popular one states that a god pulled it from his garden thinking it a weed and threw it off. It fell upside down and continued to grow, hence the name "upside down trees." In the dry season when the branches are bare, the limbs resemble roots planted in the sky. A slow growing tree in the Bombacaceae family, it is similar to its cousins, the balsa tree and the kapok tree of South America.

On the way back to the lodge we stopped on the roadside for a closer look at a flock of swallows. Everyone got out of the van and walked through the fields to get a better sighting. As I was stomping through the middle of the cornfield, I looked down and noticed how the soil was as sandy as a beach. It dawned on me as I stepped on one of the corn plants, that the field had likely been plowed with a donkey and a single-blade plow, and that every corn plant must have been planted by hand. One cornstalk might provide several ears of much needed food for the family who lived here, and here I was tramping through this family's cornfield. I was embarrassed to be so thoughtless as to assume that I could walk through a farmer's field and damage his crop, and a little surprised that the farmer did not come running out, shouting and chasing us away. But I suppose tourists are accommodated in this part of the world no matter how rude and inconsiderate they are.

Continuing eastward, we left Namibia and entered Botswana. At the border and the quarantine station we stepped through a solution of bleach (protective measures for hoof and mouth disease) and milled around while our guide filled out the necessary paperwork. All along the slopes of the floodplain, baobab trees were a welcoming green. From the border we traveled on to Chobe National Park, Botswana's most eminent national park.

Since we had driven much of the day getting to Chobe, I opted out of the evening drive. But when everyone came back with tales of a young male elephant challenging the van and nearly charging it, I was sorry to have missed out on the excitement. Chobe is known for its high concentration of Kalahari elephants (about 50,000) built up since 1990 from a few thousand, a great story of successful conservation of these elephants, the largest of the elephants. Populations of African elephants (there are two species, forest and the larger savanna elephants) have been dev-astated by poaching, and the latest rise in poaching in the early 2000s because of the demand for ivory products has resulted in a 65 percent decline of forest elephants. Savanna elephants have suffered a similar fate—populations have gone from 1,200,000 in 1980 to 430,000 in 2014. The Nature Conservancy estimates that African elephants, whose conservation status is considered vul-nerable, may become extinct within twenty years.

The morning drive in Chobe began like a poem. The hills blushed with the blooms of the Rhodesian teak trees (*Baikiaea plurijuga*), pools of standing water were pink with teak blossom reflections, and the sky was morning rose. It was as if the whole world was "a rose is a rose." The teak tree is ideal for this habitat because it's a legume and puts nitrogen back into the sandy soil, which is known for its mineral deficiencies. High populations of ele-phants in such a small space have had a heavy impact on the teak trees (as well as the other vegetation of the park), and grazing damage was obvious all along the roads. Not only the trees, but vines and any bush that looked green had been stripped of their leaves by hungry elephants.

Crossing the open grasslands and woodlands to the river's edge, we pulled off for a breakfast snack. Our guide noticed two prides of lions slinking around the distant forest edge keeping a safe distance from us as we drank lukewarm coffee and munched on cookies. A loud roar from one of males seemed less like a threat than a complaint and a reminder of how vulnerable these cats are. Estimates suggest there are only about 20,000 lions left in Africa ("Beyond Cecil: Africa's Lions in Crisis," report by Panthera and WildAid, 2016). The report claims that since the 1950s the populations of lions have dropped from 200,000 and are expected to drop again by half over the next two decades.

The riverbank vegetation of fan palms, papyrus reeds, and marsh grasses offered a shading green gazebo as we watched the syrupy brown waters making their way to the Kalahari Desert. In the middle of the desert, the river would end as it evaporated in the desert air. On the lookout for African wild dogs (the park is the last refuge for this endangered species whose numbers have declined to less than 2,000), we had no luck, but packs of banded mongoose roving the red sandy roads provided ample distractions.

The final leg of our African safari was the World Heritage Site Victoria Falls. From Chobe National Park, we traveled on well-constructed roads to the junction of the Chobe and Zambezi Rivers, ferried across into Zambia via a small speedboat and were transported by a bus the rest of the way to a lodge on the Zambezi River. Like the many dozens of lodges in the area, ours was a huge Victorian-looking hotel with accommodations for hundreds. Victoria Falls was a bit of a disappointment because all we got for our efforts was soaked, and weren't able to see much in the way of views except mist and rain. The riverboat rides on the mighty Zambezi River were another story. A morning cruise through the marshes with its ark of grazing hippos, elephants, and crocodiles gave us great views and even with the large number of tourists onboard, it didn't seem especially crowded. The evening boat ride took us closer to the falls where the river spray rose as mist and formed a huge cloud above the horizon.

Carmine bee-eaters buzzing on the banks building nest holes, and fish eagles perched like a Mother Superior in a white habit looking with concern down on the mess of the world, were fitting sights for the last event of our safari.

Victoria Falls was not as crowded as I expected. Because it is one of the most popular tourist destinations in the world, I expected hordes. With over 300,000 visitors annually at the end of the 1990s and over a million per year expected in 2018, with tourist attractions like bungee-jumping, gorge swings, cable glides, rafting, helicopter rides, and many dozen of hotels, shops and package tours available, it's likely to become more impacted by tourists in the future.

It was not until we were catching our flight home that the crowds seemed more evident and we waited in long lines with other tourists. It was a reminder of what supports much of the conservation efforts in many African countries—tourist dollars. Of all the countries of Africa, Namibia's conservation record is one of the best. Nearly 46 percent of Namibia is currently under conservation (Stoddart 2013) while Botswana has 40 percent in conservation. E. O. Wilson's "Half Earth" proposal (Hiss 2104, Wilson 2016), the policy that defines the goal of setting aside half the earth as permanently protected areas for the ten million species other than humans (hence the slogan "half for us and half for them") looks close to a reality in Namibia. In addition to the twenty-six parks and reserves, there are seventy-nine community-based conservancies that cover about 17 percent of the country. They are not parks, because people live there and raise livestock and crops, but the residents have set aside a portion of their land exclusively for wildlife (Gabel 2011). But it is the game parks that attract the tourists and generate the greatest financial incentive to conserve. "The link between conservation and tourism was the paradigm shift," writes Chris Weaver, World Wildlife Fund managing director in Namibia (Stoddart 2013). Ads touting "great safaris," "untamed wilderness," "extraordinary wildlife," are all over the media and Namibia has become one of the most traveled African countries. While the tourist model for conservation has drawbacks, the reality is that the financial incentive that drives these protected lands is tourism. In a world where one species of animal goes extinct every 10 minutes, I suppose we cannot afford to be purists. We must do whatever it takes to protect the habitats of our vulnerable species and if that means tourism, so be it.

FORESTS

CHAPTER 16.

El Paujil Reserve: Colombia

The afternoon we arrived at the El Paujil Reserve, the snake was just off the trail leading up to our cabin. Thick as the large end of a baseball bat, ten feet long, and black with yellow stripes on its head, it was a boa. Crossing a deep gully on a wobbly two-board plank bridge and climbing up a steep muddy hill, we dropped off our bags in the cabin and returned to the palaca for lunch. As we dined on pumpkin soup, we watched that snake slither up one of the palaca's posts and wrap itself around the peak of the thatched roof. For days, it lay coiled there, catching and eating bats. The morning we left it was still there.

We were part of the Traveling for Conservation program with Erin Lebbin from the American Bird Conservancy (ABC), Juan Caicedo from Fundación ProAves/Ecoturs, and a couple other birders. It was especially rewarding to travel with Erin and Juan, whose work with ABC and ProAves was making significant strides in Columbian conservation. ProAves owns and manages nineteen reserves in Colombia and, in partnership with ABC, its mission is to support and conserve habitats where biological diversity is threatened. Established in 2004, El Paujil protects one of Colombia's most vulnerable ecosystems, the rain forest of the Quinchas Mountains in the Magdalena River Valley. As of 2017, the reserve totals 8,448 acres and serves to protect many endangered and endemic lowland forest species, plus migratory birds such as the cerulean warbler, the scarlet tanager, and several other neotropical species.

It took several days of travel to get to the reserve. The journey went like this: we flew from the United States to Bogota with an overnight in the mile-and-a-half-high city. From Bogota another flight took us to Medellín where a hired van picked us up and drove us along a white-knuckle winding mountain road to Puerto Boyaca. Puerto Boyaca is located in the lowlands along the Magdalena River, and the overnight in a small local motel was a hot and steamy affair. From Puerto Boyaca to the village of Puerto Pinzon, another van hauled us up an even narrower winding dirt road through the steep foothills of the Serranía de las Quinchas Mountains. The final leg from the village of Puerto Pinzon to the reserve was a harrowing six-kilometer ride in a four-wheel drive jeep up a steep mountain mud road. Being crammed in the jeep like sardines was actually a practical arrangement because we didn't bounce quite as much when we joggled up the road, a road whose angles were sometimes as steep as forty-five degrees and whose ruts ran over a foot deep. I imagined myself being flung out of the vehicle at every turn but being jammed together kept us somewhat anchored. By the time we reached the reserve my insides felt like mush.

The drive from Medellín to the preserve crossed the Magdalena Valley, a region that has a long history of agriculture. The valley is the place where Europeans first encountered the potato, and as a highly fertile valley, it is the source of much of Colombia's produce today. The region is also infamous for its history of danger and violence. Thirty years ago it was the location of the world's largest illicit coca cultivation and cocaine production (Bowden 2001). Home of drug lord Pablo Escobar, and paramilitary and guerrilla groups such as FARC, ELN, ERP and M-19, this part of Colombia has seen terrible conflicts. Estimates of as many as three million displaced people from 1996 to 2005, and a death toll reaching close to half a million made it one of the most dangerous places on earth. While the Cali and Medellín drug cartels have been largely destroyed, hundreds of drug smuggling organizations still operate in Colombia today mostly in remote regions, primarily in the southwestern part of the country. That a simple plant, the coca plant (*Erythroxylu* species) could be turned into a commodity whose distribution and illegal use has created such terrible human carnage and corruption, has a certain sad and ironic twist for those of us who love and study plants.

Located between two mountain ranges of the Andes—the Cordillera Central and Cordillera Oriental—the Magdalena Valley is cut by the Magdalena River, which flows 700 miles and empties into the Caribbean Sea. Unlike many river valleys, this valley's terrain is not flat or smooth. Ancient sediments deposited during the Pleistocene plus eroding floodwaters have created an unusual landscape of steep mounds and deep gorges. Haciendas and cattle farms with smooth-skinned red and white Brahmas that graze in the lush green hilly pastures give the landscape a contrasting appearance, pastoral and wildly rugged jungle. These pastures were once pristine rain forests. Now clearcut for timber and pastures, they are the dominant feature of the landscape. Estimates suggest that since the 1950s nearly 98 percent of these lowland rain forests have been destroyed and that only small pockets of primary forest remain.

A lunch stop at a roadside diner along the Magdalena River provided sandwiches and lulo, the popular tangy fruit drink that comes from a species of plant in the nightshade family (*Solanum* species). It did not escape my notice that this plant does not have the chemistry of the coca plant and luckily does not run the risk of becoming part of illicit drug production. On the wires crossing the river, forked-tailed flycatchers balanced like open scissors and saffron finches flashed deep yellow. Gray-breasted martins zoomed about seining the air for insects, which were quite plentiful along the warm humid river.

Beyond the turnoff to Puerto Boyaca about midway up the mountains, a large hacienda provided what I thought was to be a short leg-stretch until our guide whispered, "blue and yellow macaws!" I have never been much of a fan of parrots. Loud obnoxious birds seen mostly in cages, in zoos or as pets, they have never had much appeal. I have read and admired Bruce Barcott's (2008) *The Last Flight of the Scarlet Macaw: One Woman's Fight to Save the World's Most Beautiful Birds* but I never particularly related to parrot-like birds nor did I understand why so many folks found them exciting. My attitude changed during that stop. In a pasture with a small creek running through it, a dead palm tree rose forty feet in the air and leaned sideways like a skewed telephone pole. Near the top, two birds peeked out from a dark hole. As they crawled out of the nest hole and clung to the side of the trunk, I was awestruck. They were enormous (over 30 inches long) and when they flew to a tree farther back from the road, they looked like angels! Blue satin, the color of the sky, and golden undersides flashed, the color of sun-lit ripened wheat fields—I was stunned by their beauty. The pair joined half a dozen other macaws perched in the trees and as we watched them, I understood why Sharon Matola would put her life on the line trying to save these birds, and why other biologists and conservationists have been trying so hard to save this threatened species. They were glorious! In their natural habitat, in their home, they struck me as sacred.

On to the preserve, we traveled through uninhabited terrain, arriving late in the afternoon. Our first evening was restful and leisurely after the long journey. After dinner, we casually hiked one of the trails to a high clearing and watched the sun set over the green, jungled hills. The preserve is about half original rain forest and half second growth. Several small flocks of parrots, the blue headed, the red lored, and the yellow crowned, flew overhead while the call of a barbet echoed in the distance. On the way back to the lodge, we stopped to see two young blue-billed curassows, or paujils, the namesake of the reserve, in their cages. Having been bought from a local villager as young birds, they were now reaching adult age. The size of small chickens, they fluttered and flew about their small cages obviously dissatisfied with confinement, typical teenagers. Attempts would be made to acclimate them to the wild, but none of us believed they had much chance of survival. Remaining in captivity did not seem like a good plan either, but I think we all hoped that if released they might remain close by and perhaps become protected lodge residents. Blue-billed curassows are the world's most critically endangered species of cracid, the avian family that includes the large turkey-like birds such as guans and chacholacas. There are only about 250 to 1,000 blue-billed curassows left in the world.

The trail back to the lodge was lit with fireflies whose lumines- cence seemed as bright as flashlights, and the sound of cicadas and frogs was as pleasing as an orchestral tune-up. The path to our cabin was steep, and while the steps were reinforced with bamboo stakes and a bamboo hand rail, in the dark, it was a bit tricky. I was also glad that we knew the snake was in the roof of the palaca.

Earlier that day, as we had stepped onto the balcony to look over the Hermit River, the scene was as lush a green tangled web as one could imagine. Palms and lianas, shrubs and vines, broadleafed trees, and even a strangler fig made up the forest's network. The fig's host tree had almost disappeared but it still propped up the duo, doing splendidly well in its rain forest home. Looking into that collection of a gazillion trees, I joked, "I spy something green."

The rain woke us up around midnight, not as a soft patter, but as a deafening roar. For hours it poured, then came down in buck- ets, then poured some more. Clashes of thunder and flashes of lightning rivaled a rock concert. By 4 a.m. it was still pouring rain, and I wondered if we would be stormbound. By daybreak the rain finally slowed and became a soft patter. By breakfast, it was gone and a different music settled over the forest. Under the dripping canopy, a mist rose through the wet sparkling branches and the roar of rushing water became more intense. The river had turned into a torrential flood of fast-moving waters. The color of melted caramel, the river's currents ran high, thick, and strong. Deep eddies formed around fallen trees and whirlpools spun around the bends. A morning walk along the river trail was still and quiet except for the roar of the river; it was as if the birds had not yet dried out or recovered from the night's storm. A few flycatchers perched in the rain-drenched branches of bamboo but not much else was moving. We would learn later from one of the forest guards of a spectacled bear that had ambled along the trail but had disappeared into the dense bamboo before anyone in our group got a good look. Some of the bamboo trees were enormous, with trunks a foot or more in diameter. Some had been cut, others were broken off, and in the bowls left by the cutting, pools of water teemed with life. Ferns and frogs and all sorts of creatures lived in these tiny bamboo aquariums.

We spent the afternoon under the palaca watching the wildlife on parade. Toady tyrants flickered in the bushes, and hummingbirds darted about the feeders. As many as ten species of hummingbirds buzzed and chased one another, clicking their beaks like fencers at swordplay. The most common species were the white-necked Jacobin and the rufous-tailed hummingbird. The fruiting palm tree next to the kitchen served as a diner whose dinner bell rang out "come one and all, soup's on!" as white-faced capuchins and coatimundis came swinging in like the place was their local hangout. Crimson-headed woodpeckers, purple-necked fruit crows, and blue and gray, crimson-backed, and palm tanagers added to the parade. A basilisk lizard crawled out onto the lawn, raised his head like a Tour de France cyclist in a biking helmet, and gave us a wary look, while a blue morph butterfly appeared for an instant, flitted through the clearing, and disappeared so quickly it might have been Tinker Bell. Heliconia butterflies flashed red, black, and yellow as they darted among the shrubs, providing more eye-catching moments.

That night there was no rain but a full moon turned the terrarium outside our cabin into a mosaic of moon shadows. The next morning everyone mentioned disturbing dreams. I had anxiety dreams, the specific details of which I could not recall, and my companion dreamt of a child falling off a cliff. Maybe it was the full moon, or maybe the conversation Juan Carlos had at dinner when he told us about the thousands of car crashes on the roads of the region. He said there were more deaths from car crashes than all the fatalities from the recent war. He went on and on in graphic detail until someone finally but politely said, "Juan Carlos, maybe we ought to change the subject; you're creeping everyone out." But then the bad dreams could have been the ghosts of all the violence past.

In the afternoon our guides arranged for a wooden dugout to take us to the village where we met members of the Women in Conservation Program. Getting to the village via boat on the Hermit River was easier than the jeep ride, but river travel can be unreliable, because it depends on water levels. While the rains had initially raised the water levels, they were now falling again. We piled in and puttered downriver under a canopy that alternated between deep dark shadows and bright sun. As lianas hung down like welcoming banners and a rufous motmot bellowed out a loud river song, the line from an old poem came to mind—"the darker the shadows, the brighter the light."

The village dock was a steep, slick mud bank and climbing its slippery slope, a challenge. We encountered young men carrying heavy planks of lumber up from the river. In rubber boots or flipflops, they hauled huge four-inch thick, ten-foot long planks on their shoulders and dropped them in large piles. Lumbering the forest was the only visible signs of anyone making a living in the village. After a hot walk along streets of what resembled an old western town in a cowboy movie, we came to a tiny one-room shop, where we were greeted by Andrea Linares, the director of the ProAves Women in Conservation program.

Andrea could have been a villager herself with her long, jet black hair, black eyes, and copper skin. Her round face glowed when she smiled. She introduced us to the women and explained a little about the program. Of the fifteen women in the program, twelve were present and they seated themselves around the table in their bright white t-shirts that read, "Mujeres por la Conservación." Andrea showed slides of how the women gathered tagua seeds, dried and processed them, and sent them off to be cut. Once the pieces were cut, the women dyed and crafted them into stylish jewelry. As the gorgeous necklaces and bracelets were passed around, Andrea explained. Tagua is known as vegetable ivory because it has the same quality of hardness and beauty as bone ivory but it is a renewable resource that comes from the tagua palm (*Phytelephas schottii* or *P. tenaicaulis*). The women in the program had begun cultivating the plants to ensure a steadier supply of the seeds, and now they needed cutting tools to eliminate the middleman, who charged them too much. As Andrea explained these events, it was obvious she cared about these women and the project. She said she got goose bumps talking about her work and that this project touched her heart.

Juan and Erin translated some of the women's stories: one woman said she had her first child at ten. Another woman was the only one who was finishing her high school degree. But the most poignant story was from a woman who told about growing up in a small village across the valley. When she was ten, guerillas came into the village and killed her brother, her father, and some of the other men of the village. The guerillas told the villagers to leave by morning or they would suffer the same fate. So everyone packed up what they could carry and fled. She had come to this village ten years ago, married a man who drank all their money away and beat her, and against tradition, she divorced him. She was trying to raise her three kids as best she could. At twenty-something, she looked a much older woman.

As we returned to the lodge from the village, the water in the river had dropped and the motor kept choking out in the mud. It had to be started again and again. When we finally arrived back at the lodge, it was nearly dark and we were exhausted, but a dinner of grilled chicken and rice and lulo revived us. After a short evening walk on one of the near-by trails for a final bird count, we turned in early.

The next morning it was time to leave El Paujil and begin our journey home. We said our good-byes and thank yous to Marta and Gloria who had cooked for us, to the forest guards, our local guide, Juan Carlos Luna, and, last but not least to the snake who still lay coiled in the rooftop waiting and waiting.

The preserve of El Paujil was as hopeful a place as any I had visited, one that proclaimed the message that a land of violence could be turned into a refuge for an endangered bird, that women from a small village could learn skills to support their families using renewable resources—making ivory jewelry from a plant seed instead of involvement with plants that become narcotics—and that tropical lowland rain forest habitats could be preserved with the efforts of professional conservationists and local residents. A model of conservation via the combined efforts of the government of Columbia, Pro Aves and the American Bird Conservancy, El Paujil was in the truest sense, a sanctuary.

CHAPTER 17.

Hummingbirds with Boots: Ecuador, Mindo Cloud Forest

The predawn streets of Quito were empty as our busload of birders left the city and climbed into the mountains. We were headed to the Mindo Cloud Forest via the birding trail known as Ecoruta el Paseo del Quinde—the route of the hummingbird. My traveling companion and I were still half asleep when one of the guides, a tall, handsome blond, blue-eyed fellow, began telling about his adventures. He had roamed Ecuador exploring for an oil company, fallen in love with the country, quit his job, and decided he would "have some of this paradise." He purchased land, built a lodge, and created a nature reserve. Half expecting his tale to be a story of redemption, perhaps like Saul on the road to Damascus, tax collector turned saint, or John Newton Clerk, slave trader turned writer of *Amazing Grace*, I imagined him a corporate oil hunter turned conservationist. What a redemption story that would be—a bright, articulate, vibrant young man becoming involved in Ecuador's conservation efforts.

When I asked if he had ever worked near Intag, a region in northwestern Ecuador where local people's conflicts with mining interests had recently been in the news, he remarked with disgust that the locals were "a bunch of leftists." Shocked by the loathsomeness in his comment, as my understanding was that the local people were working to conserve their forests—"their" being the operative word—and were attempting to create a sustainable economy, I was further dismayed as he continued his story. He explained that the discovery of any valuable commodity—whether oil, gas, copper, gold or any other resource—and its extraction resulted in changes to the community. When valuable resources were discovered, the structure of the community altered; it was inevitable that the financial, social, cultural, and power structure of the community changed. What surprised me was that he seemed to be unconcerned that such changes leave many, most often the most vulnerable, open to exploitation and that indigenous peoples were almost always the victims of multinational corporations that gained control of the commodity. Economists refer to this kind of economic transformation as "the resource curse" because while it enriches the few, it impoverishes most of the population and often leads to corrupt regimes such as Iraq and other oil-producing countries, and/or one-industry economies where the few control the commodity, the wealth of the country, and everything within the community. As the van climbed, the sky lightened and the lush slopes of the cloud forest became visible. The guide continued his monologue. Passing a village church, he remarked, "This is my church. Literally, this is my church." He chuckled. He claimed he owned not only the church, but the entire village. When he purchased the land and built his lodge, the village was part of the deal. He said the villagers paid him one dollar a year rent, a necessary precaution so that they could not claim entitlement to the land in any future land right disputes.

He told about building his ecolodge, and one morning finding a beautiful quetzal shot and hung on the lodge door. He responded by burning down the village's cornfields and letting it be known that if another bird was killed, he would burn down their homes. I don't know if his story was entirely true, but it chilled me to the bones, and I was frankly shocked by his casual brutality. He must have noticed my response because he stood up and moved to the back of the bus where he entertained the other birders with his adventures. I never interacted with him again.

The incident was a reminder that not all conservationists hold the same political beliefs as I do. Some conservationists believe the earth belongs to them and "what I conquer, or buy, I own." Peter Huber (1991: p x) describes the American environmental movement as beginning with a wealthy conservative Republican, Teddy Roosevelt, and moving to Al Gore, who Huber defines as "fusspot, curator, techno-rationalist, Kennedy School wonk." While the "wonk" label seems a little harsh, it is a reminder that conservationists hold a large range of political views, and clearly our guide fell at the right end of the political spectrum. It was naïve of me to imagine all conservationists holding liberal ideals and caring about the rights of indigenous peoples, and yet I still found it incongruent that a young man who would preserve a habitat for wildlife could treat his fellow humans with such brutality.

By the time we reached the Milpe Bird Sanctuary, the sun was up, the feeders were humming, and our companion birders, with their *Birds of Ecuador* field guides in hand (Ridgely and Greenfield, 2001), were anxious to add species to their list. Of the 350 species of hummingbirds in the world, Ecuador has 125, and the Milpe Bird Sanctuary records over 20, the little woodstar and the purple-throated woodstar prominent among them. We spotted green-crowned wood nymphs, green-crowned brilliants, rufous-tailed, and the amazing booted racket-tail hummers in their little white fuzzy Nancy boots and long wire tails. There were purple-crowned fairies, Andean emeralds, brown Incas, long-billed starthroats, and green thorntails. The air vibrated electric with the buzz of their tiny wing beats. Like their flight, the nomenclature of hummingbirds spoke to their beauty and vibrancy.

A young woman training to be a naturalist led us along one of the trails and pointed out some of the plants. As she touched a patch of lacy ground cover, the leaves curled up like a baby's hand clutching a finger. She called it the sensitive fern. She pointed out *Heliconia* blossoms and told us the white-tipped sicklebill hummingbird was its pollinator. This hummingbird's beak is perfectly designed, with a sharp downward curve just right to fit into this specific flower, which is the way with many hummers. Plants and hummers have co-evolved and over 8,000 plants depend on hummingbirds to pollinate them. Our guide told of another hummingbird that pollinates the long trumpet-like flowers in the genera *Datura*, *Fuchshia*, and *Passiflora*. The swordbill hummingbird, whose bill is longer than its body, three to four inches, is the only creature able to feed on these flowers. Just as we were about to leave, almost as if on cue a white-tipped sicklebill hummingbird flew in, slid its long bill into a *Heliconia* blossom, and began feeding.

After Milpe, we moved on to the Tandayapa Valley and the Tandayapa Lodge. Located in the Choco region of wet forests between the Andes and the Pacific Ocean, the reserve lists fifty-eight endemic bird species. We spent several hours on the trails, some steep, muddy, and a bit treacherous, spotting a few of the endemics such as a white-faced nunbird, a handful of euphonia species, and a number of others. A more relaxing afternoon, we lounged on the veranda and watched the medley of hummers at the feeders. The lodge was built on a hilltop and was surrounded by dense lush forest. Wide concrete steps led up to a veranda that encircled the main building. From the veranda the deep green canopy and several trout ponds were visible below. Swishing about the feeders were white-necked Jacobins, rufous-tailed, fawn-breasted brilliants, Andean emeralds, buff-tailed coronets, and western emeralds. One of the many privately owned ecolodges in the Mindo and Choco bioregion, Tandayapa was popular with international birders.

The Mindo Cloud Forest region boasts one of the highest species diversity in the world and active conservation efforts have been going on for many decades. In addition to private ecolodges and preserves, dozens of reserves, bird sanctuaries, gardens, and even a research center are managed cooperatively by government efforts and NGOs. The Mindo Cloud Forest Foundation lists these networks of preserves and protected lands on its website (MCF 2011). Mindo is actually the name of the parish in the Province of Pichincha whose size is about 100 square miles. Its location, nestled in the western slopes of the Andes, lies at the conjunction of two ecoregions—the Chocoan lowlands and the tropical Andes. Its elevations range from around 3,000 to 11,000 feet; it has three large rivers, hundreds of streams, montane forests, pasture and croplands, and many small villages. The variety makes for a complex landscape. From the 1970s through the 1990s massive deforestation occurred and to some extent continues today. As a result and in an effort to preserve the region's biodiversity, the Mindo Cloud Forest Foundation was formed and continues to work to protect these habitats.

Back on the return to Quito, our last stop of the day was a wayside cafe called Mirador de Rio Blancos. Perched on the steep banks overlooking the White River, the cafe was little more than a thatched roof with wooden tables, wooden slat-backed chairs, and bird feeders hanging everywhere. As we sipped cold beers, a menagerie of tanagers and hummingbirds came in from the dark branches of the cloud forest to alight on the feeders. There were flame-faced tanagers, palm, golden, and lemon-rumped tanagers, all lovely as jewels. A green thorntail hummingbird zoomed in, landed, and perched for some minutes on a feeder, its green iridescent head gleaming, turning a multitude of shades in the sunlight. As I watched the small bird balancing its body in relation to his long wire-like tail, I wondered, how anyone could kill such a lovely creature or imagine such a creature belonging to him.

The following day our busload of birders was off to Yanacocha, an hour north of Quito. The bus once again climbed up and into the mountains on a narrow winding road. Off the pavement, an even narrower dirt road crossed open grasslands and climbed higher and higher until it reached a clearing. This was the trail-head of a two-mile pathway that ran along a ridge overlooking the volcano Pichincha. The green slopes of the cloud forest at 11,000 feet were breathtaking not only because of the crisp air of high altitude but because the view was an aerial wonder. Wisps of clouds nestled in the groves of a contiguous forest that lay over miles of mountainous terrain like a blanket, with patches of *Polylepis* forests covering the slopes. Yanacocha is one of several reserves owned and managed by Fundación Jocotoco (FJ, 2011). Established in 1998 to protect Ecuadorian birds and biodiversity, the foundation consists of around 34,500 acres, and 10 reserves, and has partnered with the American Bird Conservancy, World Land Trust—U.S. and UK, Rainforest Trust, and 30 other smaller conservation organizations.

The trail was a botanical delight. Nectar plants in the genera *Bomarea, Centropogon, Fuchsia, Macleania,* and *Palicouria,* some in bloom, and the plant *Gunnera* with its prickly platter-like leaves lined the trail. At trail's end a feeding station had been set up and we ate lunch amidst the pantheon of hummers zooming in and out of the feeders. Buff-winged star frontlets, rainbow-beaded thornbills, a swordbilled, the great sapphire wing, two species of puffleg, the sapphire-vented and golden breasted, and two species of flower piercers, the glossy and masked, made their appearances. The critically endangered species that every-one wanted to add to their list, the black breasted puffleg, was not around.

I did not fully appreciate the disappointment of some of the birders when we left without seeing the black breasted puffleg until later, when I learned how rare the bird was. There are about fifteen species of these high-altitude pufflegs, but the black breasted is found only here along the ridge-crest of this volcano and only 160 to 250 individuals remain in the population.

Because the top of the ridge is flat and good for cropland, these ridge-crest habitats are rapidly disappearing. Like all pufflegs, the black breasted is characterized by dense, white feathery tufts on its legs, but its body is mostly black, with a greenish iridescence around the crown and back and a deep blue forked tail. The bird migrates in a vertical manner, being found in April to September at 7,000 to 9,000 feet, and above 9,000 feet from November to February where it feeds on fuchsias and ericaceous trees (BirdLife International 2013).

The remarkable thing about the trail was not only its spectacular beauty but also knowing that conservationists who have preserved Yanacocha and other nearby land acquisitions through Fundación Jocotoco were rescuing this very rare bird from certain extinction. Fundación Jocotoco also protects over 800 other species of birds that make their homes in these Andean habitats.

The next several days were filled with travels to even higher Andean regions. At Papallacta—elevation 14,000 feet—we watched a viridian metal-tail hummingbird feed on fuschia blossoms. The little hummer moved constantly from thicket to blossom and back again in the cold, thin air of the paramo. At Antisana Ecological Reserve, 13,000 feet, we strolled through the home of the naturalist Alexander von Humbolt, where he supposedly wrote some of his many works proposing the theory that species distribution is determined by gradients in latitude, elevation, and isolation. The cozy hacienda was built of sundried brick with a straw ceiling, and its majestic position isolated high in the thin Andes air seemed the perfect place for proposing and establishing the science of biogeography. On yet another high-altitude day, we traveled the Avenue of the Volcanos, joining a section of the old Inca trail that led to Cotopaxi National Park, and walked a barren rock trail on the slope of the volcano Cotopaxi.

As our days in Ecuador came to an end, I thought how remarkable this country of many ecosystems. It was inspiring to experience firsthand a country whose its vast biological wealth is being so well preserved. Ecuador, the size of Colorado, ranks in the top ten most ecological diverse countries in the world, and through the efforts of conservationists and the country's hundreds of reserves, it is likely to remain so. There are more than 200 environmental groups working in Ecuador dedicated to sustainable development and the country's 2008 constitution grants constitutional rights to nature (Lewis 2016).

Of course, there are never any guarantees in the fight to protect vulnerable species and it is a never-ending battle to protect lands. Oil discoveries in the Yasuni National Park in eastern Amazonian Ecuador have created a great deal of political maneuvering designed to open the park for oil drilling, and conservationists, environmentalists, and biologists are concerned about how this region—recognized as the most biologically diverse spot on earth—will be affected. When I think of the appetite of our resource-hungry world where habitats are destroyed because of oil, mineral, and timber extraction, where forests are turned into pastures for raising cattle, and the results are species extinction, I wonder if we don't need more redemption in the world. Certainly the conservationists who have worked and are still working to preserve the many ecosystems and habitats of Ecuador are enacting stories of true redemption.

COLD LANDS

CHAPTER 18.

Riding the Ring Road: Iceland

The flybus into Reykjavík hummed along a black paved highway through miles of lava fields covered in blooming lupine (*Lupinus nootkatensis*). The lupine's deep purple cone flowers created a sharp edgy landscape against the sharp, black lava rock. Nootka lupine (a species native to Alaska) was planted all over Iceland in the 1940s in an attempt to stabilize the soil, speed up land reclamation and help with reforestation. But like kudzu, that notorious plant "that ate the south," it has spread everywhere. While it has made Iceland's soil more fertile—as a nitrogen fixer that adds nitrogen to the soil, it has displaced native plant communities such as moss-heaths and dwarf-shrub heathlands. The ecological lesson we don't seem to learn is that introducing a species to solve one problem often results in creating more problems.

Shaped like an amoeba with many pseudopods, Iceland has many peninsulas that originated as lava flows oozing to the sea—and some still do. John McPhee (1989) describes how engineers and town folks fought one such lava flow after an eruptive fissure in 1973. The eruption sent molten rock towards the village of Vestmannaeyja and its port, threatening to engulf the coastal village in liquid fire. Massive amounts of sea water were pumped onto the lava to cool it, and the village was saved by sheer effort. Icelandians are a hard-working, determined folk, and this hot lava flow was only one small battle in the continual struggle against adverse weather and fault-line geology.

The lava fields of the Keflavík peninsula had long ago flowed and cooled, but a different kind of transformation seemed to be going on. While lupine was reclaiming the soil, but also becoming a troublesome invasive, bulldozers and cranes were building new houses and offices, and sprawl seemed to be transforming the landscape. I wondered if there was anywhere on earth not being altered by development.

Reykjavík is a modern, but very expensive city and our hotel accommodations, which resembled a freshman college dorm room, cost a small fortune ($500/night). Fortunately, our two guides, expert naturalist/birder, Mark Suomala, and a local driver, Siegfried, knew the country well and had planned local lodging and exploring the island with a mind for modest expense.

Our group gathered, and our journey began in a cold rain. The road to the Snæfellsnes Peninsula along the west coast of Iceland swept through a landscape of meadows and mountains. Even in the dreary rain, the scenery was drop-dead gorgeous with vivid green fields cut by rushing streams, and emerald mountains that sloped up to raw, charcoal peaks. At the small fishing village of Grundarfjörður, our hotel was near the docks. Johanna, the young woman who owned the hotel and also ran the local youth hostel, invited us on a walk-about, so we followed her like ducklings as she described the slow intimate pace of her town. Strolling pass the fish houses where tons of cod, whiting, and pollack were landed and processed, along a short block of shops, and through her neighborhood, we ended up in her church. Everything was neat, clean, and orderly. Many of the houses were constructed of corrugated iron, a design common all over Iceland because of its durability to withstand harsh weather. When we passed a house whose backyard was adorned in bright hollyhocks, Johanna remarked with perhaps a little envy in her voice that Mrs. Greenthumbson (made-up name) always had the best garden in town. A carload of teens cruised by, honked, and she waved. She laughed and explained that everyone knew everyone in town and folks loved to drive up and down the main street as a social event; it was their main form of entertainment. Inside the Lutheran church—nearly everyone in Iceland is Lutheran—she pointed out the stained-glass windows done by an artist whose name was typically Islandic, a guttural-something-or-other ending in "son." At the end of the tour, she stood beneath the stained-glass window with the late afternoon sun streaming in and sang an old, Icelandic hymn that captured the spirit of the village. It was a melancholy song; it may have praised the strong connections of village life, but it also spoke of the loneliness and limitations of small town living and the longing to escape.

The following day, the Snæfellsnes Peninsula offered Iceland's newest park. Established in 2001, Snæfellsjökull National Park is one of three national parks. The other two are Thingvellir, a World Heritage Site, and Vatnajökull, the largest national park in Europe, making up 13 percent of Iceland's territory. There are also 102 protected areas created by the Iceland's Nature Conservation Act of 1954. Snæfellsjökull National Park is about the size of Maine's Acadia National Park, 42,000 acres; it stretches from mountain top to seashore; and it has one of the most diverse geologies of any park in the world with mountains, volcanos, a glacier, ice fields, lava fields, caves, craters, streams and waterfalls, sea cliffs, and bizarre rock formations.

For a country the size of Kentucky, with a population of less than a third of a million, Iceland's parks and protected lands reflect a remarkable record of conservation, although there have been some set backs, such as the resumption of whaling. Iceland's history of whaling has been a complicated one, and a source of great conflict. Iceland originally followed the recommendations of the International Whaling Commission and issued a moratorium on commercial whaling in 1986. But after a seventeen-year moratorium, the Iceland Fisheries Ministry issued a permit in October, 2006 allowing commercial whaling to resume. Called deplorable by environmentalists ranging from Greenpeace to the World Wildlife Fund, the legalized killing of endangered fin whales clearly reflected a lack of both "wisdom and restraint" —"wisdom and restraint" being the recommendation made by Barry Lopez (1986) for preserving earth's cold lands and cold waters. As of 2015, licenses continued to be issued and whaling continues to occur. The Huffington Post reported that the June, 2015 season was allowed quotas of 154 fin whales and 229 minke whales. That trend continues to be the rule of law.

The perimeter highway known as the ring road follows the island's rocky coastline and offered many pull-offs to observe the sea and check the cliffs for sea birds. The rocky cliffs teemed with fulmars, kittiwakes, Atlantic puffins, razorbills, black guillemots, and thick-billed murres—all species of conservation concern. A few skuas glided about looking to steal the catch of an unsuspecting bird.

Among the lava rocks tough little alpine plants grew. Several in our group were especially skillful at identifying them, and with each stop, both our bird list and plant list expanded. From thrift (*Armenia maritima*), a scraggly needlegrass that sprouted pink clover blooms, moss campion (*Silene acaulis*), crowberry (*Empetrum nigrum*), lady's mantle (*Alchemilla alpina*), mountain avens (*Dryas octopetala*) to over fifty species, our list got longer. Hardy plants growing low to the ground gripping the earth as if it was a matter of life and death, they were typical of vegetation exposed to long-term frost. Mark's excellent field guide, *A Guide to the Flowering Plants and Ferns of Iceland* by Hördur Kristinsson (1998) provided photos and an easy key, so we were constantly passing the book back and forth. Hundreds of true mosses, liverworts, and lichens also inhabited the lava. With nearly 600 species of bryophytes, a similar number of lichens, which represents nearly twice the number of vascular plants, and over 1,200 species of fungi, we longed for a field guide to Icelandic's non-flowering plants, but such a guide would probably have been thicker than a New York City phonebook.

One of our fellow travelers, Sharon, walked up to the edge of one of the cliffs to take photographs. The nearness of her stand evoked such a wave of anxiety that I had to look away so as not to scream in alarm. I have never outgrown my fear of heights, and those cliffs were sheer drop-offs plunging hundreds of feet down into a foamy sea that lifted the waves and smashed them on the rocks, sending plumes of white spray high into the air. There was something about Sharon, not just her daredevil quality, but a deeper sense of boldness that made me think of the Viking woman, Gudrid, whose bronze statue we had seen earlier that day. Standing on a Viking boat with her son perched on her shoulder, Gudrid looks out onto the windswept meadow longingly to the sea. In *The Far Traveler: Voyages of a Viking Woman*, Nancy Marie Brown (2009) describes the life of this daring woman born on the Snaefellnes Peninsula around 985 AD. Living a life of hardship, Gudrid crossed the north Atlantic eight times, helped founded the first settlement of Vinland, outlived several husbands and lived to be sixty-five, a hardy old age for that time.

Formidable women seem to be the rule in Iceland, as exampled by the country's former president, Vigdís Finnbogadóttir (1980-1996). The world's first elected woman president, Ms. Finnbogadóttir was educated at the Sorbonne and was noted for her staunch support of women's rights and environmental protection. Like Norway's former Prime Minister, Gro Harlem Brundtland, whose environmental records formed the ground work for many progressive international green policies, these Nordic countries seem to grow wise and intrepid women leaders.

Our next venture, a ferry crossing to Flatey Island and Flatey

Nature Reserve, was a miserable hour and a half of rough seas. Swells ten to fifteen feet high made everyone aboard queasy. But sea sickness is remarkably transient, and as soon as the rocking stopped, recovery came quickly and with cups of hot tea from the old village café, we were soon walking the island's protected lands. All forty-plus islands and inner coastlines are part of the Breiðafjörður Bay protected area established in conservation in 1995. The cold rain stung and the wind never subsided, but the ground did not move, and two red-necked phalaropes, no more than ten feet from our path, provided an immediate distraction from the rough ride and the lousy weather. A tiny church on the hillside contained a mural that made the rocky voyage worthwhile. In the mineral colors of the surrounding mountains, a fisherman and his wife were portrayed seated on stools cleaning fish. The Spanish artist-turned-Icelandic-citizen, Baltasar had thrown his vision of the island onto the walls and ceiling of the tiny church. In the style of El Greco's "Toledo," the painting held a dark, intense sky contrasted by oystercatchers, butterflies, a white-tailed eagle, sheep, and other grounded images of the island. It was a visual hymn of praise for that tiny remote island in the middle of the arctic bay of Breiðafjörður.

The ferry ride back to the mainland was worse than the crossing. The waves had grown higher, thirty feet swells, and some of us couldn't keep lunch down. Shivering on the cold deck, I tried to focus on the horizon. Up and down, then way up and down, the horizon moved. That roller-coaster ride seemed never to end, but when it did, within minutes of reaching Stykkishólmur port, the nausea disappeared. Mark and Sigi pronounced the town, "sticky-shoal–mar," and whenever they pronounced the name of the town, its happy sound made me smile. When we arrived at the stillwater harbor of Stykkishólmur, I smiled even more.

Iceland roads are generally narrow, and in that region of the country, they are especially thin with barely enough room for two small cars. The shoulders often dropped off into either a stream, a cliff, or some other steep depression. So when a little white car approached our van taking his half more in the middle, Sigi had to swerve to avoid hitting it. The van left the pavement, hit the soft mud and gravel of the shoulder, and sunk deep into the mud. At least we didn't turn over, Sigi said, as he tried to get the van out of the mud and back onto the road. But at every attempt the tires dug in deeper, and no amount of accelerating or gunning the engine back and forth would get the van back onto the road. With a deep sigh of frustration, Sigi motioned everyone out. He asked us to stomp on the ground to pack the soil as he hauled out a rope. He attached it to the front of the van, everyone grabbed a section of the rope, and on signal, we pulled. With a collective heave-ho and with Sigi gunning the engine, the van came free of the mud and rocked back onto the road.

Someone began humming the old Willy Nelson tune, "On the Road Again" and we continued on our way with a sense of accomplishment and camaraderie. Some miles ahead at a desolate wind-blown spot a historical marker described the first settlers of Iceland. The sign read "874 AD first settled by Scandinavian Vikings." In Icelandic history, the first few centuries were known as the Saga period and involved characters like Eric the Red, Thorsteinn the Foul, Glum the Skull Splitter, and Gunar the Unwashed, to list a few, implying a time of vile, unsavory characters (Millman 1990). According to Sigi, Eric the Red's father was kicked out of Norway for manslaughter and moved to Iceland when Eric was ten. Like father like son, Eric grew into a quarrelsome fellow, and after some involvement with a killing or two, he was also kicked out of Iceland. He moved on to colonize Greenland, and his son, Leif Ericson, went on to discover North America, or Vineland as it was known to the Vikings.

Sigi rambled on and on, recounting some of the old Norse sagas as he drove in the gray mist, but I was able to catch few of the details of a rather complicated folklore. Sigi reminded me of the character Bjartur, who appears in the Noble Prize winning novel,

Independent People by Halldor Laxness (1946). Bjartur recites poetry and recounts the old legends as he wanders about in blizzards and endures the dreadful Icelandic weather looking for lost sheep. Sigi's versions of the old legends seemed to be about blood feuds and bad-tempered heroes. His long-winded narrative of two foster brothers who fought over a beautiful woman and one was killed, then the surviving fellow was killed by another family member, seemed full of contradictions, and I wondered if that was not the way we always know the past, through a mixture of legends and stories, collages of facts and fiction, confusions and contradictions. But, I suppose, if there was an overlying theme of Icelandic history it was one of settlers obsessive with independence and survival.

That evening our dinner was haddock in a thick cream sauce followed by a creamy dessert. I waddled off to bed hoping the next day would bring a little sunshine. Drifting off to sleep at the end of that gloomy day, I thought of the poem, "The Farmer in Wet Weather" by Iceland's 19th century lyrical poet, Jónas Hallgrímsson (2000). He wrote,

> *Goddess of drizzle*
> *driving your big*
> *carload of mist*
> *across my fields!*
> *Send me some sun*
> *and I'll sacrifice*
> *my cow...my wife...my Christianity!*

The next morning was nearly full sunshine—perhaps reciting the poem had appeased the goddess—and we began our travels to the northern coast. A rock island offshore from the village of Grundarfjörður (Sigi called it Church Island) was covered with angelica (*Angelica archangelia*), a plant resembling hogweed or King Kong-sized Queen Anne's lace in the parsley/carrot family. Interspersed among the angelica was the plant known as roseroot (*Rhodiola rosea*) with its yellow-green succulent blossoms giving the mountainsides and sea cliffs the look of a cultivated rock garden. In the early morning light, the landscape glowed malachite, the shade of light passing through a Tiffany stained-glass lampshade.

The northern countryside was even more spectacular than the west coast. Against wide-open meadows and green mountains, the bird life was stunning. Whooper swans speckled the fields and on one fjord, they dotted the waters like tiny white caps. Golden plovers, whimbrels with turned-down beaks, and black-tailed godwits (an endangered species) were common in the fields, and red knots perched on fence posts like hood ornaments. Harlequin ducks colored the fast moving streams in their paint-by-number colors, and eider ducks congregated in quiet coves like mismatched shoes—the male being a saddle oxford; the female, a brown hush puppy. Two white-tailed eagles perched on a distant boulder so still they may have been wrought-iron sculptures.

In a valley outside Akureyri, our lodge provided yet another spectacular postcard view. Considered Iceland's northern capital, the city is surrounded by snow-capped mountains. At the southernmost end of the Eyjafjörður fjord and with the Greenland Sea in the distance, it was an arctic landscape of majestic proportions. Looking up into the glaciers that oozed down the mountains, the descriptions of Gretel Ehrlick (2001) in *This Cold Heaven: Seven Seasons in Greenland* came to mind: "the whole mountain was one quivering mass,…chrome and slate, a mirror that did not reflect. It was rippled-buttered, then smoothed. Bits of rubble skidded down sleek walls…glaciers trying to get down were wheels churning in place, endless turning verbs with no nouns to push around."

In the early evening a short-eared owl hunted the marshes behind the lodge. He swooped low among the grasses like a giant gray moth, working his way along the edges of the fields, and finally disappearing into the mist rolling in from the sea. The winnowing of snipe was a haunting sound as the bird's display involved a downward dive repeated time and again against the backdrop of mountains and fjord meadow. The courtship display of the male snipe is produced by a high climb upward and a kamikaze plunge downward. When air rushes through the tail feathers, it produces a flappy–buzzing sound, a kind of huhuhuhuhuhuhuh. The faster the bird goes, the higher pitched the drumming, and those snipe were singing like sopranos.

The next morning Lake Mývatn—a well-recognized RAMSAR site of international important wetlands—provided a lesson in population explosions. Aptly named "lake of midges," it was teeming with flies. The moment the doors opened, the van filled with their irksome little cellophane wings. Even with netting over our heads, the insects never seemed discouraged and managed to get in and under our nets. Although they were not the biting kind, but rather small gnat-like insects called chironomids, there is something exasperating about flies up your nose, in your ears, and stuck on your teeth. I keep reminding myself they were a significant food for breeding birds, arctic char and trout, and that biologists studied their cyclic outbreaks and population crashes with great interest. However, it did not alleviate their annoyance, and I was relieved to move on to less fly-infested places.

Along the road to the ferry that would take us to Hrisey Island, a chain of mountains cut by glaciers rose from the tundra. For the first time, I understood the meaning of the geological term "hanging valley." The valleys sat high above ground level suspended in mountain ridges. This country was truly a geologist's heaven, with hanging valleys, glaciers, fjords, volcanoes, hot springs, all the formations on a movable feast of a geologically active landscape.

Unlike the first ferry ride, this one was only ten minutes and the seas were calm. The island is completely under conservation and a well-marked trail encircling the island allowed us to hike its three-mile circumference. Several arctic terns nesting in the heather just off the trail dive-bombed us, believing we were a threat to their chicks. The birds' deeply forked tails twitched like wicked scissors as they hovered in the air, and we tried to scurry along so as not to disturb them any more than necessary. This remarkable species of tern is on the endangered species list, and with good reason. It circumnavigates the earth, flying from the arctic to the Antarctic each year in one of the most amazing marathon migrations on earth. As I watched the birds hover above us like tiny angry kites, I wondered how a creature so small and delicate could fly that distance year after year—some live to be thirty-four years old. When one calculates an average bird's mileage, it's over three-quarters of a million miles on the wing. Truly remarkable!

As we walked we inadvertently flushed rock ptarmigans and they flew up from the heath with a rustle and rattle. This appaloosa, chicken-size bird was once hunted by Icelandians for Christmas dinners, but when their populations plummeted, conservation legislation was enacted to list them a threatened species and they have recovered somewhat. Circling back to the dock, we caught the last ferry back to the mainland, and returned to our lodge with a sun that followed us, never dropping below the horizon.

For three sunny days, the northern coast was our stomping ground. Most of the time we spent in the field, but one afternoon we visited the city of Akureyri driving by the docks and through the city's neighborhoods, with a quick walk-through in one the old churches, the botanical gardens, and some of the shops. A cozy corner bookstore offered a stark contrast to the vast remote landscape. There is something about a bookstore that brings the feel of civilization to a place. Iceland has the highest literacy in the world (100 percent), the lowest crime rate, and the most progressive social laws, all this I learned by browsing through the books in that bookstore.

Leaving the North country, we made our way across the island to the southern coast. The interior road was impassable; ice still covered the roads so we back tracked and cut through the edge of Iceland's cold, flat interior. Mile after mile where nothing grew, where rocks and more rocks were the only things to see, we jostled and jolted along a rutted road through a terrain as desolate as the moon. When we reached Thingvellir National Park, we were greeted by a rift valley landscape. The mid-Atlantic ridge runs through the region and separates North America and Europe. As the road twisted through the remarkable terrain, Sigi kept proclaiming in his loud sing-song voice, "now we are in Europe; now we are in America; now Europe, now America." Only after what seemed hours of his recitations did we notice Helka, a large volcano, as a distant white hump, with her head in her own cloudy breath. The region was one of active tectonic plates, and volcanoes and geysers dotted the landscape.

A monastery-turned-guest-house in Shalhots provided lodging for the next few nights, and each evening after dinner, we walked the rolling grasslands in hopes of spotting an arctic fox, but for all our efforts, we were never able to spot one. The region was full of majestic waterfalls, craters, glaciers, wild rushing rivers, and lakes. Thingvellir Lake, the largest and most popular with anglers, supports a rare Arctic char and four species of trout. Its surface mirrored the awesome cloud windrows of the Icelandic sky. At the Langjökull glacier, we watched a team of ice hikers decked out in climbing ropes and cleats coming down off the glacier. Near Gullfoss, just off the pathway, a small colony of purple stalked frog orchids (*Coeloglossum viride*) stood in juxtaposition to an enormous waterfall. Halos from the sunlight passing through the spray decorated everything in rainbows. In a nearby wetland meadow adjacent to a pasture of grazing Icelandic horses, we discovered heath-spotted orchids (*Dactylorhiza maculata*). Our plant list was by this time enormous.

One afternoon, a birch forest interspersed with rowan and willows provided us with a shady picnic spot, but the term "forest" seemed a misnomer. The original forests of Iceland were cut down long ago by early Icelandians; and while the first attempts to reforest the island began in the 1920s, the Icelandic Forest Service began more concerted efforts at reforestation in the 1990s. These forests all over Iceland are now young ecosystems consisting primarily of native birch (*Betula pubescens*) and exotic Siberian larch (*Larix sukaczewii*). Norway and Sitka spruce (*Picea abies* and *P. sitchensen*), Alaskan black cottonwood (*Populus trichocarpi*), and a number of other imported species have also been planted. The trees are generally not much taller than about fifteen feet, so the term "forest" seems a stretch. All forest canopies on Iceland are generally low and, in truth, seem more like shrub vegetation. Barry Lopez (1986) in *Arctic Dreams: Imagination and Desire in a Northern Landscape* describes typical native arctic trees, limited by available light and water, as diminutive. With pencil sized trunks and only inches tall, Arctic willows and birches that look like ground cover can be 200 year-old trees.

"The country that planted trees" seemed a good description for this island nation, but, of course, there are always critics. One of the guides leading a group of British birders who joined us one evening at dinner complained that he did not like the forests. He said they broke up the open landscape and altered the species of birds. He claimed that the tree species planted were not indigenous, and that conservation efforts were all done in too haphazard a fashion. His arguments were impressive, and as a naturalist, he was well informed in the principles of ecology, but I thought, who could really disapprove of trees, even if some of them were dwarfs and plantation trees destined for harvest and commodity. As long as they were alive and green, I loved them. For most of us, there is just something comforting about trees.

The coast of Vík offered beaches of white sand and smooth grey flat stones. The pebbles clicked like poker chips when we walked on them. Fulmars and puffins nested on the cliffs, turning the rock walls into a busy air terminal. Sea birds soared in and out, coming and going, back and forth, from rock to sea, sea to rock cliffs. Some perched on the ledges while others floated like carnival ducks on the waves beyond the breakers.

We did not travel any further east than Vík, but if we had, we would have encountered the controversial Kárahnjúkar dam and hydroelectric project. Numerous articles in the popular media have described the events surrounding this project (Swan, 2004; Lyall, 2007; Guidice, 2008) as does the book, *Dreamland: A Self-Help Manual for a Frightened Nation* by the Icelandic author Andri Magnason (2006), and several documentary films, among them "MegaStructures," produced by the National Geographic Channel, and "Extreme Engineering," by Discovery Channel.

Briefly, the story goes like this: The hydroelectric plants were being built by Landsvirkjun, Iceland's National Power Company at the demand of Alcoa. Alcoa, a subsidiary of the multinational Bechtel, made a deal with the Icelandic government to construct an aluminum plant if Landsvirkjun would provide the electricity. Bechtel is the same company that took control of the water system in Cochabamba, Bolivia, and increased the cost of water to the poor residents; the company has billions of U.S. dollars in military contracts in Iraq and Afghanistan; and the CEO, Riley Bechtel is the 127th richest man in the world according to Fortune Magazine. Landsvirkjun is owned by the State Treasury, the city of Reykjavík, and the township of Akureyri—the project to build several hydroelectric plants cost several billions of taxpayer dollars. Five dams in all, the largest one across the Jökulsá á Dal, a highlands river that springs from the glacier Vatnajökull, would result in the Halslon Resevoir, a flooded area covering fifty-seven square kilometers. It would impact one of the largest wilderness heath lands in Europe. Four other dams and two other reservoirs would also be constructed.

An environmental assessment study reported that the biggest dam would impact 3 percent of Iceland landmass and affect a number of endangered mosses and lichens, at least 280 species of small animals, and two never previously reported species of insects. The Alcoa aluminum smelter would also generate tetrafluromethane and hexafluromethane, green house gases that are over a thousand times more heat-trapping than carbon dioxide. Many Icelandic citizens expressed outrage at these corporate dealings, calling it the worst environmental scandal in Europe in 100 years, and demonstrations held world wide, and environmentalists from Iceland Nature Conservancy (INCA) and International Rivers Network (IRN) protested the destruction of the heath lands, but it did not make much of a difference. Using intimidation tactics, the voices opposing these projects were largely suppressed, and construction of the dams continued. The company and supporters of the project used the argument that 400 jobs and spin-off industries would be created and the economy of a depressed region would be improved.

On September 28, 2006, the gates of Kárahnjúkar dam were closed, and the waters rose to 559 meters as of November 29, 2006. By June 22, 2007, the Halslon Reservoir was half full; by October it was twenty-five kilometers long and one kilometer wide. The fight to save the highlands was over, and the hopes of saving this wilderness were drowned as the waters filled the Halslon Reservoir. According to some environmentalists, other corporations are lining up for the cheap energy produced by the hydroelectric dam (see website http://www.savingiceland.org). Full operation of the Alcoa plant in Reyðarfjörður, and the two other smelters were in full operation as of April, 2008.

I had to wonder, if a country with the highest literacy in the world, some of the best environmental policies of any country on earth, and enlightened human rights laws could fall prey to the manipulations of multinationals, what chance did less progressive nations have of avoiding such exploitations? It is not as if Iceland was a poor nation whose citizens needed electricity to heat their homes–there are enormous natural resources available for heat and electricity generated from thermal sources. Nor was it that the aluminum plant would provide jobs or great economic growth. The hydroelectric plants were solely being built so that Bechtel could profit. I wondered if there was anywhere on earth where the grip of these corporations did not extend, where they did not wreak havoc on native habitats, turning the good earth into aluminum cans or some other frivolous commodity.

The last day of our journey, Sigi drove our band of travelers to the Keflavík airport through the southern coastal lava fields. For miles, the gray, moss-covered lava fields stretched out like a soft baby blanket. We ate lunch on the rocks among sheep grazing on a windy hillside overlooking the sea. With mountain peaks behind us, the sea in front and the mossy lava rocks below, we all agreed the country was truly an arctic paradise.

Waiting for our flight home, I wondered if Iceland's citizens who once fought so valiantly against the goliath lava flow would be wise enough and politically astute enough to stop powerful multinationals who destroy habitats and use tax-payer money to do so. I wondered if this country, a country of immense natural beauty, whose record of environmentalism and conservation has been so progressive, would let its rivers and lands be turned into electrical generators that did not benefit its citizens, but rather made a wealthy corporation even richer. Would Iceland remain an arctic paradise, become a corporate handmaiden, or some hybrid in between? These questions may be the most relevant social/economic/environmental issues facing the world today. What seems most significant about my Icelandic journey was that it raised the question that if the rich and powerful few win here, is there hope for anyone? Would the country's financial crisis of 2008-2011 so damage the economy as to make it more vulnerable? Would this arctic paradise, like so many places around the world, especially the cold lands where shale gas extraction is becoming a reality, become a vanished ecosystem? Would Iceland become another paradise lost?

CHAPTER 19.

Boreal Forests and Arctic Tundra: Finland and Norway

Helsinki is a cold city, even in midsummer. So to spend the afternoon exploring the capital and largest city in Finland before heading off for the Arctic Circle, we had to bundle up. Near Kauppatori Square on the waterfront, a hearty seafood soup took the edge off the cold wind blowing in from the Baltic Sea; the Academic Bookstore offered a good browse; and the Rock Church with its copper ceiling and un-worked rock walls provided near-perfect acoustics for piped-in sacred music. But it was the Helsinki Central Railway Station with its art deco architecture that evoked the wow factor. A copper-green clock tower and four mythical giants known as "the stone men" flanked the arched entrance. Carved from rose-colored Finnish granite, they stood holding spherical lamps welcoming the traveler. With sharp angular cheeks and square jaws, their chiseled features were Nordic archetypes.

The flight from Helsinki to Oulou took us to the Gulf of Bothnia near the Swedish border where we met Toni Eskelin, our Finnish guide—tall, handsome,who looked a little like one of the stone men of the railway station. With Toni and Jan Hanson, our American guide, our group of birders would travel north to the Arctic Circle and then onto the Norwegian coast, which geographically bends over northern Finland like an awning. The drive would take us through arctic habitats, the taiga or boreal forests, beginning with tall canopied forests, progressing to shorter and shorter trees, through the treeless tundra of the Varanger Peninsula, and finally to the stark fjordal coast.

Before we left Oulou, the wetlands of Liminganlahti accorded us an afternoon of leisurely birding. Part of Natura 2000's network of protected areas (Natura 2000 is Europe's most renowned nature and biodiversity project), Liminganlahti is a RAMSAR site, and Finland's most important wetlands. The 30,000-acre, mostly privately owned reserve provides habitat for over 100 species of nesting birds, and as many as 250 species can be seen in the area over an annual cycle. The shallow waters of Liminganlahti Bay off the Gulf of Bothnia support reed and sedge beds and are the summer breeding grounds for the whooper swan, the common crane, greylag geese, and dozens of species of waders. The duckboard trails meandered through grass beds and along the shore with five watch towers and various bird blinds scattered throughout. Chatting sedge warblers, two soaring white-tailed eagles, and a boreal owl sitting near her nest box were among the many species we noted.

Several pairs of whooper swans feeding in the shallows near one of the blinds were also a nice sighting. The whooper swan is the national bird of Finland, appearing on its one-euro coin, and represents a successful comeback story in Finnish conservation. In the 1950s populations had dwindled to fifteen breeding pairs. Through a campaign of active protection and conservation, the numbers today are around 1,500 pairs. Wintering in northern Europe and eastern Asia (winter populations there are currently about 40,000), some migrate to northern Finland arriving in April. They then breed, raise four to seven cygnets, and leave, some as late as November. Whooper swans mate for life, are quite protective of their broods, and emit a deep whooping call from which their name derives. Seeing these enormous birds and imagining the energy it must require to raise young ones and make their migratory flights over a twenty-six-year span, I was not surprised at how seriously they fed.

On one of the trails, a greenish broken egg, perhaps that of an eider duck, lay nestled in the grass, and I remembered reading *Kalevala*, Finland's national epic poem first compiled by Elias Lonnrot in the 19th century. Like the *Iliad* or *Beowulf*, the folk poem recounts the legends and myths of the old Viking gods and their doings. In the poem, the creation myth tells how the earth was created from the shards of a duck egg, and I thought how many of our old stories and tales involve birds and animals of the natural world, and how few of our modern stories do, except perhaps in children's literature. I wonder about this relationship, how the loss of our connection to nature's creatures seems not only in fact, but also in fiction.

From Oulo we traveled northeast to Kuusomo near the Russian border and Oulanka National Park. Located near the Arctic Circle, this Lapland park is Siberian taiga, with immense forests of tall evergreens. Of the twenty species of trees, the most common are the Siberian and Scots pine (*Pinus sibirica* and *P. sylvestris*), Siberian and Norway spruce (*Picea obovata* and *P. abies*), larch (*Larix gmelini* and *L. sibirica*), and fir (*Abies sibirica*). Walking the spongy trails, we came across fairy slipper orchids (*Calypso bulbosa*) and watched a flock of Siberian jays being their usual noisy-jay selves, while overhead ravens glided the thermals in large loopy circles. Siberian jays are drab brownish gray birds with long tails and are known for their boldness and fearlessness. A characteristic known as sticky tongue allows the birds to produce a gluey saliva that binds berries and other morsels together. They can squeeze their food into compact balls and stick them onto branches or lichen clumps—I imagine them like a breakfast bar. The jays are a species typical of old-growth boreal forests (nearly 10 percent of Finland's forests is old-growth), and while populations are declining slightly, they are still considered a nonthreatened species. Ravens, on the other hand, are the smart wise guys on the bird block. Finnish ice fishermen have reported ravens lifting the fishermen's lines to retrieve the bait while the men were off warming up. Pulling the lines up and then standing on them to keep them from sliding back into the water takes a certain cleverness and agility. But such are the antics typical of ravens.

From Kuusomo north to Ivalo, Urho Kekkonen National Park offered more boreal forests. The indigenous Sami people, also known as Laplanders, raise reindeer as a traditional source of livelihood, and several small herds were feeding on the fruticose lichen known as reindeer moss (*Cladonia rangifrina*) along the roadsides. None of them had red noses, but many had large healthy racks of antlers and heavy, shaggy coats. These were not the wild Finnish reindeer which number less than 2,000, but the domestic herds numbering around 207,000 that are managed by the Sami people, who now use ATVs and snowmobiles. These reindeer were probably part of the herds the Sami were moving to their summer grazing grounds on the fjords.

It might be easy to romanticize the Sami, but the reality is that every nation devastates its native cultures, and the Finns have been no exception. In *The Magnetic North*, Sara Wheeler (2002) tells of the disintegration and cultural collapse of these people. Her stories and observations recount the past fifty years with especially heartrending observations not only of the cultural devastation but the environmental catastrophe as well. With toxic pesticides and radioactive materials contaminating their diet of reindeer meat as well as their environment, their plight is a sad one.

It was in these forests that we saw the great owls of the arctic, the northern hawk owl, the great grey, the Eurasian pygmy, and the Ural owl. They were added to our bird list because Toni knew where to look and where their nest boxes were located. While

Finland has no real mountains, the terrain is not exactly flat. A couple days of walking these boreal forests slopping through the uneven boot-sucking ground gave me an appreciation of those who work in these great cold, wet woods. Finland is the most forested of the European countries: 74 percent of Finland is forest, with 60 percent of the forests privately owned by families—one million Finns are estimated to be forest owners directly or indirectly—and its economy is heavily dependent on its forests. And the biological community certainly depends on them as well. Boreal forests, while often thought of as species poor, actually harbor more than 20,000 species of plants and animals. While these forests are not rainforest, they do have a large contingency of species and a significant biodiversity. Finland's National Forest Program is recognized as one of the world's best for comprehensive and effective policies based on sustainability.

As we continued north, we saw a roadside sign that read "The Arctic Circle." We then crossed the border into Norway and made our way onto the Varanger Peninsula. The pines and spruce disappeared and were replaced by forests of short birch (*Betula pendula* and *B. pubescens*). Soon the birch disappeared and we were on the vast treeless tundra. The transition from boreal forests of huge evergreens to short stubby birch to treeless tundra in a matter of hours was one of the most immediate and remarkable visual examples of the relationship between temperature and flora—the colder the climate, the smaller the plants was clearly observable.

Because it was early June, the tundra still had large patches of snow whose melting produced streams and rivulets all along the edges. Shallow pools formed where hundreds of seabirds, arctic ducks, waders, and shorebirds fed. Birds of prey on the prowl flew low and rapidly over the long rounded ridges looking for lemmings, voles, and slower birds. The landscape was truly thrilling! Never had I seen such vast contrasting patterns of white snow and dark heath land. A well-built paved road ran for sixty miles through arctic tundra, under a gray sky in a landscape of mires and moors to the fjordal coast. That a landscape with so little color could have such an infinite variety of shades of black and white and gray and could be so stunning spoke to the concept that beauty can be textural alone.

After arriving at the village of Båtsfjord on the Barents Sea, we spent several days exploring the coast and Varanger Peninsula National Park, which comprises a substantial part of the peninsula. The vegetation, classical heath tundra, was low, evergreen berry-bearing shrubs, such as cloudberry (*Empetrum* species), mosses (*Dicranum* species) and lichens, plus numerous grasses and sedges. Dwarf willows (*Salix* species) and dwarf birch (*Betula* species) grew shrunken and withered like bonsai. One afternoon, a bluethroat provided a bit of entertainment with its song and dance, calling and displaying in the branches of a roadside birch. About the size of a small robin, the bluethroat is an old world flycatcher in the thrush family whose bib of rusty and black crescents and bright blue throat give it a cheery appearance. In this neutral landscape where even the sky is almost always gray, the luminescent blue was a welcome splash of color.

The town of Båtsfjord is a cruise-ship village with shops, a couple of museums for visitors, and passengers roaming about from the incoming ships. The first night—"night" being misleading, as it was always daylight—around 3 a.m., I couldn't sleep, so I walked down to the hotel lobby intending to stroll the village, which turns out to be a common practice among the residents and visitors in the long daylight hours. One of my traveling companions, Tom, was down there too; he couldn't sleep either, so we began swapping Christmas stories. Because we had seen herds of reindeer and a potbellied fellow sporting a long white beard, Christmas seemed to be the running theme of the day. We had joked and laughed at our silly Christmas remarks, and Tom and I seemed determined to continue. I told a story about the Christmas I was ten and wanted a red Schwinn bike, a cruiser with red handlebars. I got a watch. Tom told one about asking for a fashion design kit and getting a chemistry set. He said he blew up the basement as revenge. I followed that with a tale of Christmas Eve when I was a graduate student getting so smashed at a Mississippi River levee bonfire that I didn't remember driving home. I hadn't realized the potency of the homemade moonshine they were passing around. It tasted like the familiar smell of benzene but because I worked in a microbiology lab, a lot of things smelled like that and I ignored the warning signs. At nearly 180-proof, it didn't take many swigs to induce the worst headache I had ever had the next day. Then Tom told about a friend of his who died of AIDS. All that the fellow wanted for Christmas was a Teddy bear, and Tom spent days trying to find one that looked like what his friend had described. Tom found one at long last in an antique store but when he went to the hospice to give his friend the bear, his friend had died. At that point, we thought we had better stop with the stories. They were getting too maudlin, maybe because of the gloom of the twenty-four-hour gray skies of mid-summer, and it was getting late. Before wandering off to bed, we decided that Christmas was not our favorite holiday and it certainly wasn't what it was cracked up to be. But regardless of our personal disappointment at Christmases past, the fact remains that many of our holiday icons originate from these Nordic countries. From Santa Claus, Saint Nick, and Father Christmas who lives at the North Pole, to reindeer that pull his sled, they are all part of the North American Christmas tradition. And neither one of us had any clue as to why that was.

As the time came to leave the tundra and make our way back to Oulou, then Helsinki and home, I asked Toni how Finns typically celebrate Christmas, thinking they might decorate trees and give gifts. He replied that his friends gather, drink a little salmari, take saunas, and talk; the lovely phrase he used was "talking the world into a better place." With about 16 percent of its total landmass in protected areas, thirty-five national parks, nineteen nature reserves, and twelve wilderness areas plus small local reserves, the Finns have an excellent record of conservation and environmentalism, and the country ranks among the best in the world (Lyytimäki 2007). From managing its forests to protecting biodiversity, Finland has enacted progressive conservation policies. Norway has a history of sound environmentalism as well, but Friends of the Earth Norway (NNV), that country's oldest environmental and protection organization, has warned that companies eager to tap the rich undiscovered oil deposits and natural gas reserves of the Barents Sea will certainly impact the region (Allen 2012). I could only hope that Toni and his friends' strategy for talking the world into a better place would be enough to ensure that these arctic lands and wildernesses remain pristine. I could only hope that talking and storytelling would lead to better conservation. How lovely to think that we might live on words alone, and that they could actually make a better world.

CHAPTER 20.

Roots: Wales and Scotland

There are places anchored in our hearts not only by where we have lived but by the stories told by those we love. Such was the idea of Wales, for my Nain ("grandmother" in Welsh) was born on the Llynn Peninsula in Pwllheli, and grew up in Beaumais before immigrating to the United States as a young woman of nineteen. She told of Wales as a mythical place of her childhood, and when I was a little girl, she gave me a doll dressed in traditional Welsh costume. The doll had a full black skirt with petticoats beneath, an apron over it, a loose-sleeved white ruffled blouse with a flame red flannel shawl, and a black stovepipe hat. It was the same costume I saw in a picture framed on the dining room wall in the bed and breakfast our first night in Wales in the town of Hay on Wye. When I asked Dawn Farnworth, the innkeeper of the Start, she said her Nain wore such an outfit. The image of my own Nain dressed in her shawl and long skirt rushing off to sing in the Welsh choir, perhaps to a Cymanfa Ganu, or Welsh songfest, came flooding back as sweet memories. Dawn served us laverbread (bara lawr), a traditional Welsh bread made from seaweed said to be a good source of iodine, iron, and various vitamins, and recalled that she and her Nain used to collect the seaweed together. Before we left for the day, Dawn taught me a Welsh word, "cwtch," pronounced it, and said it meant a cuddle or hug. What a sweet way to start the day: a good breakfast, the recollection of pleasant memories, and a vowel-less word to think about.

We had arrived at the Manchester Airport and were met by our guides, Ruth Miller and Alan Davies, authors of *The Biggest Twitch: Around the World in 4,000 Birds* (Davies and Miller 2010). Alan and Ruth are the notable British birders who in 2008 set a new world record for sighting the largest number of birds—4,341 in one calendar year—having traveled in 27 countries. They now have their own company that offers tours of the UK, Europe, and a number of other international destinations. Ruth is also the author of two regional guides, *Birds, Boots and Butterflies: Conwy Valley/Eastern Snowdonia*, and *Birds, Boots and Butterflies: Anglesey* (Miller 2009 a,b), which describe most of the nature preserves, birding sites, and walking trails of northern Wales. These excellent guides are valuable resources for anyone planning to travel in the area.

The road through the Wye Valley was as verdant as a nature poem, and with patches of bluebells creeping along the forest floor it was a glorious spring ride. We intended to explore the book town of Hay on Wye with its two-dozen bookstores the first afternoon, and the following day to visit Hereford castle to see the chained books. We did those things and had a hands-on experience in the chained library, where we opened several of the ancient manuscripts of vellum and textile rags that were attached to the shelves by dungeon chains. Even then it seems book thievery was a problem requiring drastic measures. But our visit to the Begwyns near Clyro provided the most lasting impression of the Welsh landscape. Narrow winding roads lined with hedgerows of pollarded woody shrubs and trees crossed pastures divided by stone fences. Many of the hedgerows were quite tall, some six feet and higher, and were composed of complex mixtures of hawthorn, hazel, wild rose, ash, holly, blackthorn, oak, willow, sycamore, rowan, and other species. Not only are these hedgerows of scenic and historical importance, well-managed hedgerows provide important wildlife habitats for birds, small mammals, and numerous invertebrates. They are widely encouraged by many conservation groups.

The Begwyns is part of the UK's National Trust lands. A high, open mound, it may have been an ancient Druid site with its panoramic views of the Black Mountains to the east, the mountains of Brecon Beacon to the south, and the rolling quilted hills of County Powys to the west and north. A grassy path leading up to the summit ended at a stone fence that enclosed a grove of trees and a stone arena. As we made our way to the top, the air was full of skylarks singing. The males, which are rather nondescript streaky brown birds with crests, rose almost vertically to nearly a hundred feet in the air, hovered for a few moments, and then parachuted back down to earth singing all the while. Their territorial displays were answered by the females, which perched in the gorse bushes and sang back. With such glorious music, who could not think,

> *Hail to thee, blithe spirit*
> *our sweetest songs are those that tell of saddest thought*
> *Better than all measures*
> *of delightful sound*
> *better than all treasure that in books are found.*

The sad element of the poem might be that skylark populations are declining, although the Royal Society for the Protection of Birds (RSPB) has encouraged farmers to leave bare patches or "scrapes" where the ground is left unplowed to provide safer nesting sites. The practice seems to be making some difference but populations are still decreasing.

The following day we were off to northern Wales and Llandudno with stops along the way at Offa Dike—it was too rainy and cold for a trek along the 177-mile pathway that separates Wales from England—the town of Knighton to watch dippers in the River

Teme, the Black and White village in Herefordshire County, and to hug an ancient oak. In Llandudno on the northern coast, the statues of characters from *Alice's Adventures in Wonderland* and *Through the Looking Glass* the mad hatter, the white rabbit, the red queen, and Alice herself scattered throughout the streets gave a clue that Lewis Carroll had some connection to this old Victorian city. While not likely the place he wrote the books, it is believed that Carroll was inspired by the adventures of Alice Liddell while on holiday in Llandudno.

We settled in at the Stellar House, a local bed and breakfast, for the night and enjoyed a hearty breakfast next morning before exploring the Great Orme. The Great Orme is a massive dolomite peninsula of limestone dating back to prehistoric times; today it is a nature preserve. The Orme is two miles long and a mile wide and boasts 431 species of rare or unusual plants. Grassland flora include the critically endangered cotoneaster (*Cotoneaster cambricus*) found only on this small patch of the world, and more common alpine flowering plants such as cranesbill, sea campion, thrift, purple orchid, common rockrose, wild thyme, and spring squill. At the cliffs, colonies of seabirds, guillemots, kittiwakes, razorbills, fulmars, and gulls gave the binoculars a good workout. Walking the old cemetery of Saint Tudno, we sighted willow warblers and ring ouzels along the dry stone fences, as well as wheatears and whinchats. Rummaging through the loose stones near the old copper quarry, we spent some time looking for crinoid and coral fossils but weren't lucky enough to find a whole specimen. The morning ended with what was to become a lovely routine, a stop at the local tea shop for tea and cake.

The afternoon's visit to the RSPB-Conwy preserve was a visible reminder of the miracle of restoration ecology. Maybe "rewilding" is not the precise term, but the idea of re-creating a natural tidal-river flat from a waste site is the same principle. The 100-acre preserve, originally a waste dump located on the

Conwy River, has been called an upside-down nature reserve because of the manner in which it was constructed. In 1980, the British government decided to build a road tunnel through the estuary to relieve traffic into and out of the old walled town of Conwy. The 3.5 million cubic meters of mud, silt, and sand left over from digging the tunnel were pumped onto the near shore, making it resemble an industrial waste site. After three years, a single warden and a regiment of volunteers turned the muddy barren into a nature reserve by planting thousands of trees, native reeds, grasses, and shrubs. Native bird species began to return, trails were made, and in 1995, the reserve opened to the public. What a joy it must have been to see the place transformed! Twenty years later, the trails are brimming with native plants, and at the Tal-y-fan hide, black-tailed godwits, lapwings, sedge warblers, and shelducks feed among the reeds and on the ponds. Across the river, the crenelated, greystone watch towers of Conwy Castle, one of eight fortresses built by Edward I between 1283 and 1289, and the six-foot thick wall surrounding the village of Conwy, designed to keep the Welsh under control, loomed fiercely against a cloudless blue sky. It was a view that made me think of good intentions, a restored estuarine habitat, and the preservation of medieval buildings perhaps as a reminder of the impermanence of political boundaries.

The Isle of Anglesey was a short drive from Llandudno and we spent several days exploring first the western part of the island and then the northern coast. Starting the morning with tea and cake in a quaint tearoom on the main street of Beaumaris, we made our way on the buzz of sugar and caffeine toward Penmon Point. The morning passed pleasantly, as we explored Llanfaes, first the Smithy Cottage where my Nain lived as a schoolgirl, restored and now listed as a "cottage of distinction" (Ty'n Refail), and then walking the cemetery of St. Catherine's looking for familiar family names on the tombstones. The phrase "keeping up with the Joneses" came to mind as we waded in the tall grass, finding the surname "Jones" carved on every other headstone. The Penmon Priory and Church was a step back into medieval times, with the ruined walls of the 6th-century abbey, the old dovecote, and the holy well dedicated to the Welsh saint Seriol. Then onto Penmon Point where Puffin Island rose from the cold gray Irish Sea like the hump of an emerging whale. The coastal path running alongshore was a good way to observe the island and so we walked. The 80-acre limestone Puffin Island is designated as a site of special scientific interest (SSSI) and as a special protected area (SPA) and has a large breeding colony of great cormorants. While privately owned, the RSPB offers pleasure cruises to the island in the summer months and in partnership with the Countryside Council of Wales (CCW) conducted a brown rat eradication program some years ago to help protect bird populations. A few puffins remain, but if any were about, they were too far away to spot. Razorbills and guillemots, and a couple of gray seals bouncing along in the gunmetal waters provided amiable and interesting sightings.

The last stop of the day was the Spinnes Reserve. Located on the Aberogwen estuary and managed by the North Wales Wildlife Trust, the small ten-acre preserve has tidal and woodland habitats. From the blinds overlooking the lagoon, we spotted widgeon, teal, gulls, and a few oystercatchers and whimbrels feeding quietly in the shallows, and when long-tailed tits buzzed in from the woods, they added a zesty liveliness to the afternoon.

The northern coast of Anglesey was another day's outing. From the town of Holyhead, to the village of Rhoscolyn, and onto to Mount Holyhead was a drive along the coast of the Irish Sea. As we climbed higher onto Mount Holyhead and South Stack-RSPB Preserve, Alan pointed out ravens and choughs flying in the open grasslands. The area is managed for choughs, a species of crow now protected in the UK. This red-billed, red-legged crow was once one of the most abundant birds in the UK, but by the 1950s populations plummeted because of egg collecting, hunting, and changes in land use. Bringing back low-intensity livestock farming and placing the bird on the Amber List (U.K.'s category of conservation importance), has led to an increase in the population, and an estimated 450 breeding pairs now live on and around the reserve.

At the car park, we got out and followed a footpath that joined the Anglesey Coastal Path. The path ran along the wild and windy sea cliffs of Holyhead and through rugged grasslands of kidney vetch, thrift, squill, and scurvy grass. Stopping to check the cliffs and rolling waters below, we noted razorbacks, guillemots, fulmars, and a few common black puffins bobbing about in the waters and coming and going from the rocky ledges. A group of birders had gathered with scopes and cameras to observe the nest of a peregrine falcon. The bird seemed to be quite the celebrity on this lonely stretch of coast, with its troop of onlookers.

Peregrines are one of the best illustrations of successful bird conservation. These raptors were almost decimated in the United States and the UK in the 1940s and 1950s as the result of DDT and other organochloride pesticides. U.S. populations had dropped by nearly 90 percent and the bird was placed on the endangered species list. After 1972 when DDT was banned, their numbers climbed from 324 breeding pairs to 3,000 in the United States. The UK now has 1,500 breeding pairs. Perhaps the love affair people have with falcons was the driving force in the preservation of the bird. As a sport, falconry dates back to at least 2000 B.C.E., and those who have embraced falconry range from medieval English and European kings to Shakespeare to modern-day ornithologist Tim Gallagher. While the literature on falconry is extensive, one of the most beautifully written contemporary pieces is Helen Macdonald's (2014) *H Is for Hawk*. The story of her taming a goshawk is both a memoir of the relationship between a person and a hawk and a meditative tome on overcoming grief. It exemplifies the British love for and obsession with birds.

Leaving the car park, we made a quick stop at the hut circles, ancient stone foundations dating back to the Iron Age, around 500 B.C.E., and then headed down the mountain to Holyhead Harbor for a close-up glimpse at black guillemots. Paddling along with an occasional flash of vivid red feet, the bobbing guillemots avoided the incoming and outgoing ships and the ferry to Ireland with great agility. Then we were off for our much welcomed tea and cake at a local teashop.

The next several days were devoted to exploring Snowdonia National Park. One of Europe's great national parks, it covers over 800 square miles, and has habitats ranging from rugged mountains to quiet lakes, woodlands of deciduous forest and conifer forests, to wild grassy moorlands. Managed by the Snowdonia National Park Authority, the park is 70 percent privately owned lands, 16 percent Countryside Council for Wales (CCW) lands, and 9 percent National Trust lands. Our first outing began with a visit to the thirteenth-century church of Saint Mary in Caerhun. Morning dew sparkled on the ancient yews surrounding the church, and beyond the stone fence goldfinches flittered in the bushes. As the sun warmed the air, peacock and red admiral butterflies appeared, and a couple of lambs frolicked in the meadow. It was as sweet a pastoral scene as one could imagine, and it was easy to understand how Romantic poetry originated from such landscapes.

The path up the Aber Valley in the Carneddon Mountains must be one of Wales' most idyllic walks. The nature reserve managed by the CCW is a two-and-a-half-mile footpath along a stony creek to a waterfall. The creek banks were carpeted with great patches of bluebells and white hawthorn blossoms beneath shady old oaks and ash trees. The morning was a symphony of spring with the creek rapping in scat, a birdsong concerto in C major, and leaves bristling like the brush of snare drums. The woods, full of wood warblers, redstarts, gray wagtails, and nuthatches provided accompaniment. But it was the cuckoos calling, the achingly melancholy cries echoing off the hills that seemed to pierce the moment with awareness. Since the early 1980s cuckoo numbers have dropped by 65 percent for reasons that are still unknown, and the bird has been placed on the "red list" by RSPB (RSPB 2014). Land use changes in Africa from where they migrate, or declines in food insects in the UK may be part of the reasons, but the calls of these cuckoos were a clear reminder of the changing seasons from these birds, known as the harbingers of spring. As we sat on the rocks at the waterfall listening to the splendid sounds and watching the waters tumble over the cliff, the last two lines from the poem "A Blessing" by James Wright, came to my mind:

> ...Suddenly I realized
> That if I stepped out of my body I would break
> Into blossom.

Another day provided a different kind of forest. Gwydir Forest is national forestland that has been managed and replanted with conifers such as Sitka spruce, Douglas fir, Japanese larch, Norway spruce, and Scots pines—an internationally flavored forest. The forest was once the site of lead and zinc mines and contained many abandoned manmade lakes. As we walked around one of the lakes, we had to dodge the mechanical harvesters that were cutting trees on one side of the hill. The noise and disturbance did not make for a peaceful walk, and it was raining, but the tangy fragrance of the cut conifers was a holiday scent, and glimpses of siskins and crossbills made the trek worthwhile.

A brief stop at Pensychnant near Betws y Coed provided pied flycatchers. The 150-acre conservation center of Pensychnant was once the estate of the Stot family and is now managed as a private trust. The manor serves as a nature center, and the wooded trails provide access to forests of native oaks, silver birch, rowan, pines, sycamores, and chestnut. The European pied flycatcher, an old-world flycatcher, is not a particularly rare bird but it is an uncommon sighting. The male is such a lovely thing, with contrasting black and white markings; it reminded me of our eastern kingbird. The pieds winter in West Africa, migrate to the UK to breed in these woods, and return to Africa each year, clocking in as many as 10,000 miles per year.

From the misty conifers of Gwydyr Forest and the deciduous forest of Pensychnant, the peaks of Mount Snowdon and Llanberis Pass were a dramatic shift in habitats. The landscape became craggy with sheer rock faces, gullies, and almost no vegetation. Not even sheep grazed on the rocky slopes. With such an awesome landscape, lots of tourists were taking pictures, but when I stepped out to do the same, I was hit with a bitter cold wind that nearly took my breath away. I hurried back inside the car and we moved on. The drive down the mountain brought us back to the coast and milder climes for a walk along the salt marshes of Morfa Madryn. This nature reserve is part of three reserves established by the North Wales Coastal Conservation Partnership as "disturbance-free areas for birds" allowing birds to feed, rest, and breed along these shorelines. From several of the hides, lapwings, red-breasted mergansers, and little-ringed plovers—always nice to see—were spotted.

An evening drive along the Conwy Valley to Trefriw for dinner at the Prince of Arms Inn concluded our explorations of Snowdonia. The dinner of Yorkshire pudding, roast beef, and apple crumb was delicious English cuisine, but it was the drive along the Conwy Valley that made the most vivid impression. The sunlight streamed out of gaps in the aubergine-colored storm clouds above the hills and shone on the fields and stone fences along the river. The light illuminated the forest and the meadows, turning everything a translucent emerald. The hue evoked the magical feel of a fairy tale. The drive down the valley to the inn took only half an hour, but I wished that it would never end. It was a scene that has become etched in my memory, and I wondered if my Nain had walked this valley as a girl and been as moved as I by its sublime beauty.

A day on the Llynn peninsula and the town of Pwllheli began with our usual tea and cake at a local teashop. Ruth located and drove by the house where my Nain was born. A plain two-story row house, its steep gray slate roof, flat stone gray façade, and slate sidewalk gave it a rather drab pewter appearance. I must admit to a bit of disappointment at its ordinariness, but behind the suburban street there was an estuary and the wetlands of Afon Rhyd-hir—"afon" is the Welsh term for river. In the back-waters, a tiny local refuge, the Lon Cob Bach Nature Reserve, had paths, a wooden walkway, and a nesting of gray herons. A mother gray heron stood watch over her furry-headed chicks which occasionally peeked out from a massive stick nest. The reserve, created by the Gwynedd County Council, seemed a pop-ular place for walkers and bikers coming to and from the central part of town. Pwllheli was an old market town, and I imagined Nain as a young child perhaps going to market with her mother or playing in the tall reeds along the creek, and maybe even com-ing across the splendor of a gray heron nesting.

Oriel Plas Glyn y Weddw in the village of Llambedrog was where Nain's father worked as a coachman, and offered a peek into the life of the landed gentry. Built in 1859, the gothic Victorian man-sion was owned by the Madryn family and had been converted into Wales' oldest art gallery. With its many-roomed galleries exhibiting paintings for sale, and a collection of rare porcelain on exhibit, its staircase and decor could have been a set for Down-ton Abbey.

After a quick jaunt through the galleries, we headed for the trails. The Madryn Path through the Winllan woodlands was deeply shaded with larch and oaks and an understory of laurel, rhododendron, and wood sorrel. The path climbed to a lookout that offered an aerial view of the coast with sky blue waters, white sand, and sailboats, as pretty as a postcard. Since the walk worked up our appetites, we stopped for tea and cake in the gallery's tearoom as reward for our hard work. As I sipped my hot sweet milky tea, I wondered why we Americans seem so enamored by a lifestyle that offered luxury to only the few. This desire to be a prince or princess when young, or the lord or lady of the manor when old age sets in has always seemed an odd sort of fantasy. The fact that most of us Americans probably came from the servant class and our European immigrant ancestors made such enormous strides in the new lands of America suggests that our yearnings might be more likely a rags-to-riches fantasy. But then fantasies are illogical and probably unexplainable. It occurred to me that perhaps sanctuaries function in a manner similar to the immigrant experience, i.e., they provide places that allow room for expansion, room to grow and become successful, or even in a literary sense, a room of one's own.

From northern Wales to the Scottish highlands was about a five-hour drive, with a stop for tea and cake, of course. The Grant Arms Hotel in the town of Grantown-on-Spey is billed as UKs wildlife hotel, and it served as our base for exploring the highlands of Cairngorms National Park. The 19th-century refurnished graystone manor sponsors events for the Bird Watching and Wildlife Club (BWWC) such as guided walks, talks, and workshops, as well as briefings and information to the casual visitor. From the hotel a shortcut through back alleys took us to the Anagach Woods, where an evening stroll helped shake off the stiffness from the drive. The Anagach Woods, managed by the local Anagach Woods Trust, is a mixed highland forest with high-canopied trees of Scots pine, birch, rowan, willow, and aspen, with a scattering of hazel and juniper shrubs, and an open understory of bilberries, heather, and wood sorrel. The network of trails running along the Sprey River offered the loveliest of highland woods/riverine habitat with great woodland birding.

A morning drive through the Revack estates revealed large areas of moorlands managed for the game bird, the red grouse. Natural heather moorlands are characterized by small shrub such as ling heather and bilberry, mosses, and cotton grasses. About 38 percent of Scotland is covered in moorlands and Scotland has around 70 percent of the world's moorlands. These fragile lands are being bought up by international buyers who have been purchasing all the old estates and converting them into hunter/tourist attractions. Large patches of moorland have been burned (called muir burns) to allow young shoots to regenerate and promote habitat for the red grouse, but the controversial practice of shooting hen harriers and foxes because they are grouse predators has made this sort of management unpopular with conservationists.

A walk along the shore of Lockindorb with the ruins of a 12th-century castle on an island in the middle of the lake was a Celtic delight, but when an arctic loon—the black-throated diver—appeared, it was icing on the cake. We watched the loon feed and tried to focus our binoculars on its gorgeous black and white plumage. It was a difficult task because the bird seemed to surface for only a moment and when it appeared again, it was in a very different place.

To get to the Loch Garten Osprey Centre in the RSPB Abernethy National Nature Reserve we had to drive through an ancient Caledonia pine forest. This habitat, a Scots pine forest that once covered much of the Scottish highlands, is one favored by the capercaillie, a rare grouse occasionally seen in the area. Alan drove very slowly in hopes of seeing the bird but no capercaillie appeared that day and the forest seemed very quiet. In contrast, the osprey center was abuzz with activity. In the nature center, a large excited crowd surrounded a camcorder focused on an osprey nest. When one of three eggs began to show signs of cracking, cheers went up and clapping echoed throughout the hall. We didn't stay long enough to see the chick actually hatch, as it would take some hours, but we did get good looks at crossbills and crested tits in the trees along the pathway.

The Findhorn Valley was next on the agenda. A deep narrow valley with the swift-running Findhorn River winding through the moorlands, its steep hillsides of scraggly larch and birch had highland cattle in long shaggy coats grazing in the fields. Near a hunting lodge we paused to watch a golden eagle soaring over the mountain tops and disappearing into the next valley. Then on through Glenmore Forest and Loch Morlick, encountering a stocky red-haired fellow strolling the roadside in a kilt, we made our way to the funicular train station. The rail tram took us up to the summit of Cairns Gorm Mountain, lifting us up 4,000 feet to a stunning panoramic view of the highlands. In celebration for making it up the mountain, we had hot chocolate in the Ptarmigan Restaurant and wandered outside to watch a real ptarmigan meandering and nibbling its way among the lichen-covered rocks and low montane scrub. In the thin silent air where every shadow seemed as sharp as a knife-edge, the landscape of deep green conifer forests speckled with the silver patches of lochs seemed the very essence of the Scottish highlands. Nan Shepard, who spent her life walking these mountains, describes the light here as "luminous without being fierce, penetrating to immense distances with an effortless intensity..." and where "the height goes to one's head," and "gazing into its clarity, one loses all sense of time" (Shepard 1977: 2-3).

Before leaving the national park, we made a few additional visits: to a private pond to catch a glimpse of Slovanian grebes, golden eyes, graylegs, and Urasian wedgens; to a wildlife blind one evening to catch a glimpse of badgers, pine martens, and a tawny owl; and to a couple of small private reserves to add some of the woodland birds such as wood thrushes and willow warblers to our list.

The drive from Scotland back to the Manchester Airport was a bit somber. We said our goodbyes, expressed our gratitude to our wonderful guides, and settled into the airport hotel for an overnight before our flight home the next morning. With time to reflect on what we had seen, I took a great deal of satisfaction knowing my roots were in some of the most beautiful lands in the world and that the government and the citizenry cared for their lands. The twenty-plus sanctuaries that we visited from national parks to tiny local reserves were evidence that the lands of northern Wales and the highlands of Scotland are being protected. What better sense of pride can one hope for than to have ones' roots in a place where people believe in sanctuaries and make them a reality?

Epilogue

The question one might ask of anyone concerned with the environment is, "Why would one travel to a particular place—in my case, twenty countries in the new millennium, and why to protected areas—over sixty sanctuaries?" With all the possible actions one might take to help preserve earth's diversity—genetic banking, breeding/release programs, invasive species eradication, and all the many types of restoration ecology—why would witnessing wildlife sanctuaries, preserves, and various protected lands offer such a feeling of accomplishment? To travel long distances involves some degree of compromise, because most travel adds to the carbon footprint. Perhaps to justify that cost, something must be gained. It might be as simple and personal as "seeing is believing," or it might be the need to be around those who inspire hope and joy. Clearly, my travels brought me joy, and while some were difficult, each offered a valuable truth. Sometimes that truth was factual, such as the reality that tourism provides financial support to parks in many countries or that development is always a compromise, and sometimes that truth was an implicit sense of rightness when being with those who value and honor their lands. So many folks, not only the guides who helped me see the various countries, but the park rangers and volunteers, the people who lived in and around the refuges, and my fellow traveling companions, were compassionate conservationists who honored and valued their lands.

In the 20th century, protected lands were argued to be either "utilitarian conservationism," where parks, preserves, and public lands were used to provide sustainable natural resources, or "aesthetic conservationism," where preservation of land meant leaving the wilderness wild. In the 21st century, protected lands have taken on the larger role of protecting earth's declining biodiversity. "One of the best strategies for conserving biodiversity just about anywhere on the planet is your basic park or reserve. These are protected areas that limit or entirely exclude human access to natural resources, despite the potential impacts of that exclusion on their livelihood," writes conservationist Jason Goldman (2016). Thus, the concept of a preserve by definition has come to imply human exclusion; but the question modern refuges face today is to what degree is human exclusion necessary? The days of "fences and fines" do not work as well as more participatory conservation, and the concept of "more carrots, less stick" seems to be the current model for successful refuges.

What constitutes a successful sanctuary is complex, and the answers to the following questions might provide some insight: "What attributes do successful refuges around the world share?" "What factors temper or limit the success of a sanctuary?" "What role does the personnel and staff of a refuge play in the success of a refuge?" and, "What role does funding from varied sources such as government, private donors, and commercial tourism play?"

Just as I believe there are no failed good deeds, I believe there are no failed sanctuaries. But there are refuges that are more successful than others in protecting rare or endangered species, in keeping habitats as natural and pristine as possible, and in counteracting the ecological devastation of development. The following summarizes and gives some examples of factors that may play a role in the maintenance of a successful refuge.

The coastal waters of Tunisia are not a bordered refuge. There are no boundaries, no staff, no administration, no personnel, no funding, and yet the shoreline offers protection for migrating flamingos because the Tunisian government has enacted laws which the citizenry abides. So far, the protection of these birds seems to be working. There are many places in the world where protective laws would be difficult to enforce and depend on a compliant citizenry. Areas along the Platte River in my own country, for example, providing stopovers for the sandhill cranes on their migratory route, are privately owned. State and federal laws have been enacted to ensure that the birds are not hunted and are protected but such laws are not the only reason the birds are left unharmed. Certainly an amenable citizenry which values the birds plays a role, but the fact that the birds boost the local economy also leads to a more compliant citizenry.

Inaccessibility is a factor that becomes highly advantageous for the success of a sanctuary. One of the most remote refuges I visited was Eaglenest Wildlife Sanctuary in the Indian Himalayans. There are few facilities for visitors, getting there is difficult, and there is no infrastructure. This relatively new refuge is successfully protecting the newly discovered and most rare species of sparrows—the Bugun liocichla. Secluded Bale Mountain National Park in Ethiopia is another example of an isolated refuge providing protection for the world's most rare canid, the Abyssinian wolf. And finally, the hard to reach Laguna de los Pozuelos of Argentina is successfully protecting the four species of South American flamingos.

In contrast, many refuges are highly accessible. African game parks are heavily impacted by tourism, and while specific animals are protected, the overall ecology of many of these areas are in decline. The Galapagos, whose entire island archipelago forms a sanctuary, have also been impacted by tourism. While invasive plants and animals brought in by humans have caused the islands' ecological decline, modern tourism is clearly affecting the islands today. Many national parks, those of the U.S, as well as those of other countries, are highly accessible and claim millions of visitors annually. While the characteristic of accessibility is handled in different ways by different managements, the fact remains that tourism brings in money, and the resolution of its impact is always a balancing act and a compromise.

Other factors that play a role in the success of a refuge include size and placement. Nameri National Park in India shares a northern border with Pakhui Wildlife Sanctuary, so collectively the two refuges provide nearly 300 square miles, and with such a large land mass also serve as an effective tiger reserve. The Mindo Cloud Forest Reserves of Ecuador is another example of combining refuges and land areas to provide corridors for the protection of birds and wildlife on the western slope of the Andes. Likewise, the Mayan Biosphere Reserve in Guatemala is part of one of the largest corridors of the world, the Path of the Panther Corridor (also called the Mesoamerican Biological Corridor), covers over 300,000 square miles. Connecting protected lands in seven Central American countries, it is estimated that this corridor has saved 106 critically endangered species from extinction. The final illustration of connective conservation is the parks and reserves of southern Africa. Part of the Kavango-Zambezi/KAZA-TFCA corridor—which cover about 170,000 square miles and fall within the countries of Angola, Namibia, Botswana, Zambia and Zimbabwe—these reserves form a corridor representing one of the most successful models of elephant and large mammal conservation in the world.

As in any endeavor, financing and economics are crucial factors, and the acquisition of funding plays a role in the success of any sanctuary. The U.S. National Wildlife Refuge system, as exampled by Eufaula and De Soto National Wildlife Refuges, has been funded—or underfunded as some have complained—by the U.S. government since its inception. With annual budgets of around $500 million—$508 million was budgeted for 2016—such funding reflects a more consistent and reliable source of support, so that long term policies and projects can be more readily implemented.

Many large refuges have multiple sources of financial support, which is always a wise strategy. Galapagos National Park, for example, is funded by the Ecuadorian government, UNESCO as a World Heritage Site, the Galapagos Conservancy (formerly the Charles Darwin Foundation), park entrance fees, and private donors, as well as other funding sources. The Maya Biosphere Reserve (Tikal National Park) whose management makes use of zoning or the nesting doll approach is also funded by multiple sources: the Guatemalan government, UNESCO, The Nature Conservancy, Conservation International, and the Conservation Agreement Fund—a U.S. based non-profit. The old adage warning of putting all one's eggs in one basket might be apropos because it is always better to have diversity whether in finance or biology.

Many refuges, however, have very small budgets or none at all. The bear blinds and conservation areas in Romania have tiny budgets. Many refuges in Wales and Scotland, the yunga preserve called Huico Reserve, the Tufted Jay Preserve in the Sierra Madres of Mexico, to list a few described here, have no annual budgets and depend entirely on the dedicated efforts of local volunteers to manage the areas. Such reserves have been highly successful in protecting specific species and indigenous flora, and illustrate the philosophy of "local is always the best control."

Personnel, staff, and local support are clearly elements that play a major role in the success of any refuge. El Paujil in Columbia is funded by the ProAves Foundation in partnership with the American Bird Conservancy: it has some of the most dedicated professional conservationists, volunteer conservationists, and local participants of any sanctuary in the world; and it supports sustainable projects such as Women In Conservation, whose mission is to enhance women's economic roles. These characteristics make it one of the finest models of inclusive conservation in the world.

The protected lands described here show that actions to protect earth's biological heritage are being taken and can be taken anywhere. Every country and most every person I encountered seemed to be aware of the preciousness of their lands and to take pride in the measures they have enacted to preserve them. From large national parks managed by a country's central government to tiny reserves established and cared for by local groups or even single individuals and families, preserved lands have great protectors. The experience of seeing and walking these places has given me a great sense of hope. By sharing these experiences, it is my hope to pass such optimism on. For if the measure and meaning of our species—the species with the greatest intellect and powers of reason—is definable, it is to preserve the complexity and beauty of earth's biology and to leave the legacy of nature's value.

References

Chapter 1

Rio Electrico, Writing the River: Argentina, Los Glaciers National Park

Veblen, Thomas T., Robert S. Hill, and Jennifer Read, eds. 1996. The Ecology and Biogeography of *Nothofagus* Forests. New Haven, Conn.: Yale University Press.

International Rivers. 2009. HidroAysen Severely Flawed Environmental Study. http://www.internationalrivers.org/resources/hidroayspercentC3percentA9n-s-severely-flawed-environmental-study-3562

Chapter 2

A Place of Cranes: United States, Nebraska, The Platte River

Cather, Willa. 1918. *My Antonia*. Boston: Houghton Mifflin.

Eiseley, Loren. 1957. *The Immense Journey*. New York: Random House.

Frazier, Ian. 1989. *Great Plains*. New York: Farrar, Straus, and Giroux.

Hoogland, John L. 2005. *Conservation of the Black-tailed Prairie*

Dog: Saving North America's Western Grassland. Washington D.C.: Island Press.

Hyde, Dayton. 1968. *Sandy: The True Story of a Rare Sandhill Crane That Joined Our Family.* New York: Dial Press.

Johnsgard, Paul. 1981. *Those of the Gray Wind: The Sandhill Cranes.* New York: St Martin's Press.

– 1995. *This Fragile Land: A Natural History of the Nebraska Sandhills.* Lincoln: University of Nebraska Press.

– 1998. *Crane Music: A Natural History of American Cranes.* Lincoln: University of Nebraska Press.

– 2001. *The Nature of Nebraska: Ecology and Biodiversity.* Lincoln: University of Nebraska Press.

-2005. *Prairie Dog Empire: A Saga of the Shortgrass Prairie.* Lincoln: University of Nebraska Press.

Knopp, Lisa. 2007. "A Salt Marsh Reclamation." pp. 142-147 in *Landscape with Figures: The Nonfiction of Place.* Ed. Robert Root. Lincoln: University of Nebraska Press.

– 2002. "Affinity," pp. 41-53 in *The Nature of Home: A Lexicon and Essays.* Lincoln: University of Nebraska Press.

-2002. "Braided," pp. 74-80. In *The Nature of Home: A Lexicon and Essays.* Lincoln: University of Nebraska Press.

Lockwood, Jeffrey. 2004. *Locust: The Devastating Rise and Mysterious Disappearance of the Insect That Shaped the American Frontier.* New York: Basic Books.

Michener, James. 1974. *Centennial.* New York: Random House.

Norment, Christopher. 2008. *Return to Warden's Grove: Science,*

Desire, and the Lives of Sparrows. Iowa City: University of Iowa Press.

Olsen, Tillie. 1961. *Tell Me a Riddle.* New York: Dell.

Powers, Richard. 2006. *The Echo Maker.* New York: Farrar, Straus, and Giroux.

Savage, Candice. 2004. *Prairie: A Natural History.* Vancouver, BC: David Suzuki Foundation/Greystone Books.

Vivian, Robert. 2001. "The Tides, The Tides" pp. 90-100. In *Cold Snap as Yearning.* Lincoln: University of Nebraska Press.

Wickenden, Dorothy. 2011. *Nothing Daunting: The Unexpected Education of Two Society Girls in the West.* New York: Scribner.

Chapter 3

Along the Chattahoochee: United States, Alabama, Eufaula National Wildlife Refuge

Langley, Ricky L. 2005. Alligator attacks on humans in the United States. *Wilderness and Environmental Medicine* 16: 119-124

Lemonick, Micheal D. 2006. "Death by Alligator." *Time,* May 21, 2006. http://content.time.com/time/magazine/article/0,9171,1196427,00.html

Lopez, Barry. 1978. *Of Wolves and Men.* New York: Charles Scribner & Sons.

Russell, Karen. 2011. *Swamplandia.* New York: Knopf.

Maron, Margaret. 1997. *Killer Market.* New York: Mysterious Press.

Chapter 4

From the Himalayas the Brahmaputra Flows: India, Assam, and Arunachal Pradesh

Choudhury, Anwaruddin. 2003. "Birds of Eaglenest Wildlife Sanctuary and Sessa Orchid Sanctuary, Arunachal, Pradesh, India." Forktail 9: 1-13. http://orientalbirdclub.org/wp-content/uploads/2012/09/Choudhury-Eaglenest.pdf

Chapter 5

The Durango Highway, San Blas, and Marismas Nacionales: Mexico, West Coast

AIDA. The International Association for Environmental Defense. 2011. http://www.aida-americas.org/en/project/mexicanwetlands

Alliance of Hope Blog. 2011. http://www.allianceofhope.org/blog_/2011/12/i-will-light-candles-this-christmas.html

Gallagher, Tim. 2013. *Imperial Dreams: Tracking the Imperial Woodpecker through the Wild Sierra Madre*. New York: Atria Books, Simon and Schuster.

Kerouac, Jack. 1957. *On the Road*. New York: Viking.

Longfellow, Henry Wadsworth. 2011. "The Bells of San Blas." http://poetryfoundation.org/archive/poem.html?id=180984

Miller, George O. 2009. "A Canyon of Their Own," All About Birds. Cornell Lab of Ornithology. http://www.allaboutbirds.org/Page.aspx?pid=1421#top

Otus asio Tours. 2011. http://www.otusasiotours.com/index.shtml

Warne, Kennedy P. 2011. *Let Them Eat Shrimp: The Tragic Disappearance of the Rainforests of the Sea*. Washington, D.C.: Island Press.

World Wildlife Fund. 2014. "Southern North America: West Coast of Mexico." http://worldwildlife.org/ecoregions/rt1420

Chapter 6

Tropical Paradise: Ecuador, The Galapagos

Nicholls, Henry. 2006. *Lonesome George: The Life and Loves of a Conservation Icon*. New York: Macmillan.

Weiner, Jonathan. 1994. *The Beck of the Finch. A Story of Evolution in Our Time*. New York: Alfred Knopf.

Chapter 7

Barrier Island: United States, Florida, Amelia Island

"Amelia Island Sea Turtle Watch." 2015. http://www.ameliaislandseaturtlewatch.com

"City of Fernandina Beach Florida." 2014. http://www.fbfl.us/turtle.com

Harlan, Will. 2014. *Untamed: The Wildest Woman in America and the Fight for Cumberland Island*. New York: Grove Press.

McPhee, John. 1971. *Encounters with the Archdruid*. New York: Farrar, Straus and Giroux.

Chapter 9

Brown Bears: Romania, Carpathian Mountains

Hallab, Mary Y. 2009. *Vampire God: The Allure of the Undead in Western Culture*. Albany: SUNY Press.

Stoker, Bram. *Dracula.* 1897. London: Arthur Constable.

Slobodyan, A. A.1976. "The European brown bear in the Carpathian." Paper #32. http://www.bearbiology.com/fileadmin/tpl/Downloads/URSUS/Vol_3/Slobodyan_Vol_3.pdf

Chapter 10

The Abyssinian Wolf: Ethiopia, Bale Mountain National Park

Burrard-Lucas, Will, and Rebecca R. Jackrel, and Jaymi Heimbuch. 2013. *The Ethiopian Wolf: Hope at the Edge of Extinction*. San Francisco, CA: Lobelia Press.

Davies, Alan, and Ruth Miller. 2010. *The Biggest Twitch: Around the World in 4,000 Birds*. London: Christopher Helm.

Iyer, Pico. 2007. "Heaven's Gate" pp 23-47 In Klara Glowczewska ed. *Book of Unforgettable Journeys: Great Writers on Great Places*. New York: Penguin Books.

Johanson, Donald, and Maitland Edey. 1981. *Lucy: The Beginnings of Humankind*. New York: Simon and Schuster.

Murphy, Dervla. 1968. In *Ethiopia with a Mule*. London: John Murray Ltd.

Verghese, Abraham. 2011. *Cutting for Stone*. New York: Knopf.

Chapter 11

Mayan Ruins, Fincas, and a Quetzal: Guatemala

Conservation Magazine. 2015. A Nesting Doll Approach to Protecting Americas Wilderness. http://conservationmagazine.org/2015/07/a-nesting-doll-approach-to-protecting-americas-wilderness/

LaBastille, Anne. 1980. "A Quetzal Reserve," pp 74-81. In Assignment: Wildlife. New York: E. P. Dutton.

LaBastille, Anne. 1990. Mama Poc; An Ecologist's Account of the Extinction of a Species. New York: Norton.

Maslow, Jonathan Evan. 1986. Bird of Life, Bird of Death: A Naturalist's Journey through a Land of Political Turmoil. New York: Simon and Schuster.

Menchu, Rigoberta, and Elisabeth Burgos-Debray. 1984. I. Rigoberta Menchu: An Indian Woman of Guatemala. London: Veros.

Ward, L.K. and Green, G.T. 2015. Wilderness Zoning: Applying an Adapted Biosphere Reserve Model to Wilderness Areas. Illuminare: A Student Journal in recreation, Parks, and Tourism Studies. No. 13. http://scholarworks.iu.edu/journals/index.php./illuminare/article/view/13341

Chapter 12

The Yungas, the Chaco, and the Altiplano: Argentina, Salta, and the Northwest

Romero, Simon. 2012. "A Forest under Siege in Paraguay." The New York Times. March 25, 2012.

"Criminal Nature: The Global Security Implications of the Illegal Wildlife Trade" 2013. Report by International Fund for Animal Welfare. http://www.ifaw.org/united-states/resource-centre/criminal-nature-global-security-implications-illegal-wildlife-trade

Chapter 13

Sky Islands and a Desert River: United States, Arizona, New Mexico, Texas

Heald, Weldon. 1967. *Sky Island*. Princeton, N.J.: Van Nostrand.

McPhee, John. 1981. *Basin and Range*. New York: Farrar, Straus and Giroux.

Nabhan, Gary. 1985. *Gathering the Desert*. Tucson: The University of Arizona Press.

Quammen, David. 2004. *Song of the Dodo: Island Biogeography in an Age of Extinctions*. New York: Scribner.

Rose, Ananda. 2012. *Showdown in the Sonoran Desert: Religion, Law and the Immigration Controversy*. Oxford: Oxford University Press.

Shelton, Richard. 1992. *Going Back to Bisbee*. Tucson: The University of Arizona Press.

Urrea, Luis Alberto. 2004. *The Devil's Highway: A True Story*. New York: Little, Brown.

Chapter 14

Where the Desert Meets the Sea: Mexico, The Baja

Feller, Candy. 2007. "Mangroves in the Margins." Smithsonian Environmental Research Center Newsletter. Spring 2007. http://www.SERC.Si.edu/about/07_feller.aspx

Gilbert, Bil. 2002. "Prince of Tides: Before 'Ecology' Became a Buzz Word John Steinbeck Preached That Man Is Related to the Whole Thing." Smithsonian. Jan. 2002, vol. 32, no. 10, pp 95-98.

Jauregui, Brian and Sergio. 2013. "Balandra Bay and Felipe Calderon's last act as president." http://forums.bajanomad.com/viewthread.php?tid=67385

Krutch, Joseph Wood. 1986. *The Forgotten Peninsula:A Naturalist in Baja California*. Tucson: The University of Arizona Press.

Owl Research Institute. 2013. http://owlinstitute.org

Steinbeck, John, and E. F. Ricketts. 1941. *Sea of Cortez: A Leisurely Journal of Travel and Research*. New York: Viking.

Warne, Kennedy. 2011. *Restoring Trees in the Tide: The Ocean's Vanishing Rainforest*. Washington, D.C.: Island Press.

White, Robert. 2008. "The beach that turned back commercial tide." http://www.theguardian.com/travel/2008/may/27/mexico.beach

Chapter 15

African Safari: Africa, Namibia, Botswana, Zambia

Gabel, David A. 2011. "Namibia Wildlife Conservation." ENN-Environmental News Network—Know Your Environment. May 23, 2011. http://www.enn.com/wildlife/article/42730/print

Hiss, Tony. 2014. "The Wildest Idea on Earth." Smithsonian. September, vol. 45, no. 5, pp. 68-78.

Stoddart, Veronica Gould. 2013. "Namibia is up to its neck in rare species." The New York Times, November 22, 2103.

Wilson, E.O. 2016. "Half Earth: Our Planet's Fight for Life." New York: Liveright Publishing Corp.

Chapter 16

El Paujil Reserve: Colombia

Barcott, Bruce. 2008. *The Last Flight of the Scarlet Macaw: One Woman's Fight to Save the World's Most Beautiful Birds*. New York: Random House.

Bowden, Mark. 2001. *Killing Pablo: The Hunt for the World's Greatest Outlaw*. New York: Atlantic Monthly Press.

American Bird Conservancy (ABC). http://www.abc.org

Fundacion ProAves/Ecoturs. http://www.proaves.org

Chapter 17

Hummingbirds with Boots: Ecuador, Mindo Cloud Forest

BirdLife International. 2013. "Black-breasted Puffleg Ericnemis nigrivestis." http://www.birdlife.org/datazone/speciesfact-sheet.php?id=2033

Jocotoco Conservation Foundation. 2011. http://fjocotoco.org

Huber, Peter. 1999. *"Hard Green: Saving the Environment from the Environmentalists—A Conservative Manifesto"* New York: Basic Books.

Lewis, T.L. 2016. *Ecuador's Environmental Revolutions: Ecoimperialists, Ecodependents, and Ecoresisters.* Cambridge, MA: MIT Press.

MCF. 2011. Mindo Cloudforest Foundation. http://www.mindocloudforest.org

Ridgely, Robert S., and Paul J. Greenfield. 2001. *The Birds of Ecuador.* Ithaca, New York: Cornell University Press.

Chapter 18

Riding the Ring Road: Iceland

Brown, Nancy Marie. 2009. *The Far Traveler: Voyages of a Viking Woman.* Orlando: Harcourt.

Sola, Katie. 2005. "Iceland's Whale Hunting Season Begins Despite Global Moratorium." The Huffington Post. June 2005. http://www.huffingtonpost.com/2015/06/29/iceland-whale-hunt_n_7691636.html

Del Giudice, Marguerite. 2008. "Power Struggle: The People of Iceland Awake to a Stark Choice: Exploit a Wealth of Clean

Energy or Keep Their Landscape Pristine." *National Geographic.* March 2008.

Ehrlich, Gretel. 2001. *This Cold Heaven: Seven Seasons in Greenland.* NY: Pantheon Books.

Hallgrimsson, Jónas. "The Farmer in Wet Weather." http://digicoll.library.wisc.edu/Jonas/Dalabondi/Dalabondi.html

Kristinsson, Hördur. 1998. *A Guide to the Flowering Plants and Ferns of Iceland.* Reykjavík, Iceland: Mal Og Menning.

Laxness, Halldór 1946. *Independent People: an Epic.* NY: Alfred A. Knopf.

Lopez, Barry. 1986. *Arctic Dreams: Imagination and Desire in a Northern Landscape.* NY: Charles Scribner's Son.

Lyall, Sarah. 2007. "Smokestacks in a White Wilderness Divide Iceland." *The New York Times,* February 4, 2007.

McPhee, John. 1989. "Cooling the Lava" In *The Control of Nature,* pp. 95-179. NY: Farrar, Straus, Giroux.

Millman, Lawrence. 1990. *Last Places: A Journey in the North.* Boston: Houghton Mifflin.

Swan, Jon. 2004. "The Icelandic Rift: Industry versus Natural Splendor in a Progressive Nation." *Orion.* March/April 2004.

Chapter 19

Boreal Forests and Arctic Tundra: Finland and Norway

Allen, Daniel. 2012. "Lofoten's Troubled Waters." *Geographical.* http://www.gepgraphical.co.uk/magazine/lofoten/_-_mar_12.html

Lyytimäki, Jari. 2007. "Life and Society: Environmental Protection in Finland." http://finland.fi/Public/default.aspx?contentid=160041&nodeid=41799&culture=en-US

Wheeler, Sara. 2011. *The Magnetic North: Notes from the Arctic Circle*. New York: Farrar, Straus and Giroux.

Chapter 20

Roots: Wales and Scotland

Davies, Alan, and Ruth Miller. 2010. *The Biggest Twitch: Around the World in 4,000 Birds*. London: Christopher Helm. http://www.birdwatchingtrips.co.uk/

Macdonald, Helen. 2014. *H Is for Hawk*. New York: Norton.

Miller, Ruth. 2009a. *Birds, Boots, and Butterflies: Conwy Valley/ Eastern Snowdonia*. Llanmst, Wales: Llygad Gwalch Press.

Miller, Ruth. 2009b. *Birds, Boots, and Butterflies: Anglesey*. Llanmst, Wales: Llygad Gwalch Press.

RSPB. 2014. "The State of the UK's Birds-2014. https://www.rspb.org.uk/Images/state-of-the-uks-birds_tcm9-383971.pdf

Shepard, Nan. 1977. *This Living Mountain*. Aberdeen, Scotland: Aberdeen University Press.

Acknowledgments

Thanks go to my traveling partner, Darleen Abbott, for without her I would probably never have gotten very far, and to my cousin, Richard Lillie, for his work on the history of the Morgan family that provided places for me to trace my roots in Wales and Scotland. Special thanks go to the following guides who made my travels to the sanctuaries and protected lands described here both joyful and hopeful: foremost to Ruth Miller and Alan Davies of the Biggest Twitch; Jan Hanson of Otus Asio tours and Toni Eskelin of Finland; Denver Holt and Megan Fylling of the Owl Institute; Mark Suomala; Richardo Clark, Patricia Clark, Mauricio Clark, and Mario Mosqueira of Argentina; and Erin Lebbin of American Bird Conservancy, and Juan Caicedo and Andrea Linares of ProAves. Thanks also go to all the many rangers, forest guards, and staff of the various reserves for their generous efforts.

Index

ABC (American Bird Conservancy), 155, 163, 170, 221

Abernethy National Nature Reserve, 213

Aberogwen estuary, 206

Aber Valley, 208–9

Abies sp. (fir), 120, 195

Abra Pampa (shrine), 113

Abyssinian wolf (*Canis simensis*), 4, 93–94, 95, 219

acacia (*Acacia* sp.)

  black hook, 139–40

  of the bush veldt, 139–40

  catclaw, 126

  of Ethiopia, 91–92

  of the Galapagos Islands, 62

  ocotillo, 5, 126

  yellow bark, 139

Acacia caven (churqui), 111

accessibility, of sanctuaries, 219–20

Acorus calamus (Calamus) (sweet flag), 27

Adansonia digitata (baobab trees), 148, 149

Addis Ababa, Ethiopia, 88, 89, 93, 95

Aesculus indica (Indian horse chestnut), 41

aesthetic conservationism, 218

Afar warriors, 90

"Affinity" (Knopp), 23–24

Afon Rhyd-hir, 211

Africa. *See also* Ethiopia; Namibia

  Angola, 146–47, 220

  Botswana, 4–5, 148–50, 151, 220

  conservation in, 4–5

  Kavango-Zambezi/KAZA-TFCA corridor, 220

  tourism in, 151–52, 219

  Zambia, 4–5, 150–51, 220

African elephants, 149

Bale Mountain National Park, 4, 92–94, 95, 219

bamboo, 42–43, 160

banded mongoose, 143

Bantu, 141

baobab trees (*Adansonia digitata*), 148, 149

barbets, 158

Barcott, Bruce, 158

Barents Sea, 198, 200

bare-throated tiger herons, 56

Barranca del Liebre canyon, 53

barred owls, 21

barrier islands, 4, 69, 70–74

Basilica of the Immaculate Conception, 52

basilisk lizards, 150

bass, 104

bats, 4, 57–58, 124–26

Båtsfjord, Norway, 198–99

bay leaves, 71

The Beak of the Finch: A Story of Evolution (Weiner), 67

BEAKS, 73–74

bears
  brown, 4, 81, 83–84, 86
  spectacled, 160

Bechtel (company), 188, 190

Bechtel, Riley, 188

beech forests, Andean, 10–12

bee-eaters, 151

beetles, black ground, 22

Begwyns, 202–3

"The Bells of San Blas" (Longfellow), 54–55

Bell's vireo, 123

Bengal tigers, 44

Bertrand (steamboat), 21

Betula pendula, 187

Betula pubescens, 187

The Biggest Twitch: Around the World in 4,000 Birds (Davies and Miller), 89, 202

Big Talbot Island, 73

Big Talbot State Park, 72–73

biodiversity
  in Ecuador, 168–69, 172
  in Kaziranga National Park, 44
  protected lands and, 2, 218

Biosphere Reserves, 57, 98, 113, 134

birch (*Betula pendula*), 187

birch (*Betula pubescens*), 187

birch forests, 187, 197, 198

Bird of Life, Bird of Death: A Naturalist's Journey through a Land of Political Turmoil (Maslow), 102

chiffchaffs, 38

Chihuahua desert, 4, 119–22, 127–28

Chihuahua pines, 120

Chile, 14

Chilean flamingos, 114

Chilean flickers, 13

Chilean swallows, 9

China, 93

China-India border, 40, 42

Chinese lantern (*Myzodendrum* sp.), 11

Chiricahua Mountains, 119

Chiricahua National Monument, 4, 119–22

chironomids, 184

Chloraea magellanica (porcelain orchid), 11–12

Chobe National Park, 149–50

Chobe River, 150

Choco region, Ecuador, 168, 169

cholera, 28

cholla cactus, 126

choughs, 206–7

Christmas stories, 198–200

Church of Saint Mary, 208

churqui (*Acacia caven*), 111

cicadas, 159

cienegas, 122

Cladonia rangifrina (reindeer moss), 196

Clark, Mauricio, 107

Clark, Patricia, 107

Clark, Ricardo, 107, 108–9, 114–15

Classical Mayan Age, 100

clay dunes, 20

clear-cutting, of rain forests, 157

Clerk, John Newton, 165

cloudberry (*Empetrum* sp.), 198

cloud forests
  of Guatemala, 102

  Mindo Cloud Forest, 4, 165, 168–69, 220

  of Santa Cruz Island, 61

  yunga, 108, 110, 114

club moss, 11

coatimundis, 160

cobras, Cape, 92

coca plant (*Erythroxylu* sp.), 156, 157

Codonorchis lessonii (dog orchid), 12

Coeloglossum viride (purple stalked frog orchids), 186

coffee plantations, 54, 101, 103

cojines, 113

Cold Snap as Yearning (Vivian), 19

in Waterberg Plateau National Park, 142

wood storks as, 70

Engelmann spruce, 120

Enterolobium contortisiliqum (pacara), 108

environmental impact study, 14, 189

Epako game park and lodge, 140–42

epiphytes

of Andean beech forests, 11

in cloud forests, 61, 102, 108

in eastern broadleaf forests, 41

in mangrove swamps, 56

eradication programs, 20, 22–23, 135, 206, 217

Ericson, Leif, 181

Eric the Red, 181

Erongo, 140

Erythrina falcata (ceibo), 108

Erythroxylu sp. (coca plant), 156, 157

Escobar, Pablo, 157

Eskelin, Toni, 193, 196, 199–200

Espinoza del Diablo (Road of Three Thousand Curves), 52–54

Estero de San Jose Del Cabo State Reserve, 130

Ethiopia, 87–96

Bale Mountain National Park, 4, 92–94, 95, 219

Jemma River Gorge, 87–88, 89

Rift Valley, 89–90, 94–95

Ethiopian wolf. *See* Abyssinian wolf

Ethiopian Wolf Conservation Program (EWCP), 94

Etosha National Park, 143–46

Eufaula National Wildlife Refuge, 4, 31–35, 220

Eurasian pygmy owls, 196

evergreen oak (*Quercus devia*), 137

EWCP (Ethiopian Wolf Conservation Program), 94

extinction

African elephants risk of, 149

of the Atitlan grebe, 104

development and, 172

human wealth and, 26

of the imperial woodpecker, 55

Lonesome George and, 64

Path of the Panther Corridor and, 20

rate of, 152

risk of, 126

of the Rocky Mountain locust, 22–23

"Extreme Engineering" (film), 188

Eyjajorour fjord, 183

fairy slipper orchids (*Calypso bulbosa*), 195

falconry, 207–8

falcons, peregrine, 207

fan palms, 150

"The Farmer in Wet Weather" (Hallgrimsson), 182

Farnworth, Dawn, 201–2

The Far Traveler: Voyages of a Viking Woman (Brown), 179

fawn-breasted brilliants, 168

Federal Area of Flora and Fauna Protection, 134

Feller, Candy, 132

Fernandina Beach, Florida, 70

ferrets, 26

Festuca sp. (bunchgrass), 113

figs, strangler, 51, 102, 159

financial support, 152, 217, 220–22

Finca El Pilar, 103

fincas, 4, 101

finches, Darwin, 67

Findhorn Valley, 214

Finland, 4, 193–200

Finnbogadottir, Vigdis, 179

fin whales, 178

fir (*Abies* sp.), 120

fir (*Abies sibirica*), 195

firefiles, 159

fireland cherry lumber, 11

fish eagles, 151

fishing bats, 57–58

fish markets, Ethiopian, 94–95, 96

flame-back woodpeckers, 40

flame-faced tanagers, 169

flamingos
  Andean, 4, 5, 114
  Chilean, 114
  in Etosha National Park, 146
  at Laguna Pozuelos, 113, 114
  lesser and greater African, 76–77
  puna, 114
  in Tunisia, 4, 5, 76–77, 219

Flatey Nature Reserve (Flately Island), 179–80

flickers, Chilean, 13

floodplain forests, 20–21

floodplains, 4, 21, 43, 44, 149

Flores, Guatemala, 97, 98, 100–101

Florida
  alligator encounters in, 33–34
  Amelia Island, 4, 69, 70–74

Florida Department of Natural Resources, 72

Florida Fish and Wildlife Conservation Commission, 34

invasive species

  of bass, 104

  black hook acacia as, 140

  eradication programs for, 20, 22–23, 134–35, 206, 217

  in the Galapagos Islands, 63

Irish Sea, 206–7

IRN (International Rivers Network), 189

Iron Age, 208

irrigation, 23–24, 110

irruption, of snowy owls, 73

Isabela Island, 63

Isabela Project, 63

Isla Espiritu Santos, 134–35

Isla Pinta, 64

Isle of Anglesey, 205–8

IUCN (International Union for Conservation of Nature), 2

IUCU, 76

Iyer, Pico, 88–89

jackals, 141

Jack Sinn State Memorial Wildlife Management Area, 22

javelinas, 127

jays

  brown, 99

  Siberian, 195–96

  tufted, 53–54

Jekyll Island, 69

Jemma River Gorge, 87–88, 89

Jia Bhoroli River, 39

Johnsgard, Paul, 25, 26

Jökulsá á Dal River, 188–89

Juglans australis (nut tree), 108

juniper, 119, 126

Kaeaona, John, 146

Kalahari apple leaf, 142–43

Kalahari desert, 139

Kalahari elephants, 149

Kalevala sp., 195

Kameng Protected Area Complex (KPAC), 40

Kaokoland, 140

kapok tree (*Ceiba pentandra*), 99

Karahnjukar dam, 188–90

karst, 98

Kavango-Zambezi/KAZA-TFCA corridor, 220

Kaziranga National Park, 38, 43–45

Keflavík peninsula, 176

Kerouac, Jack, 51, 59

keystone species, 26

Khoisan peoples, 141

K'iche Maya ethnic group, 105

Killer Market (Maron), 33

kingfishers, 146

oak (*Quercus* sp.)

of Chiricahua National Monument, 120

in eastern broadleaf forests, 41

emory, 126

evergreen, 137

gray, 126

live, 71, 72

observational science, 64–65

Ocala National Forest, 33–34

ocellated turkeys, 99

ocotillo acacia, 5, 126

Odendaal Plan (1960s), 140–41

Odonatus echios (prickly pear cactus trees), 66

Odyssey (Homer), 75–76

Offa Dike, 204

O'Haile, Susan, 28

oil deposits, 172, 200

Okaukago lodge, 144

Okavango River, 146–47

Okhla Bird Sanctuary, 37–38

old-growth forests, 195

old man's beard (*Usnea* sp.), 11

olive groves, 76

Olsen, Tillie, 28

Omaha, Nebraska, 19

Omaruru River, 142

Omni Resort, 72

one-horned Indian rhinoceros, 43–44

"On the Road Again" (Nelson), 181

On the Road (Kerouac), 51

Opuntia sp., 62, 110

orange-crowned warblers, 131

orchids

of Andean beech forests, 11–12

fairy slipper, 195

heath-spotted, 187

in mangrove swamps, 56

purple stalked frog, 186

organochloride pesticides, 207

Oriel Plas Glyn y Weddw, 211

orioles, 102

ORI (Owl Research Institute), 137

ornate tinamou, 111–12

osprey, 213–14

Oulanka National Park, 195

Oulou, Finland, 193, 194, 199

Outer Banks, 69

overharvesting, 109

Owl Research Institute (ORI), 137

owls

barred, 21

boreal, 194

cape pigmy, 137

Eurasian pygmy, 196

great grey, 196

marsh, 147

Mexican spotted, 126

northern hawk, 196

pigmy, 145

screech, 115

short-eared, 183–84

snowy, 73

tawny, 214

Ural, 82, 196

oxalic acid, 141

Oxychloe andina, 113

oystercatchers, 206

pacara (*Enterolobium contor-tisiliqum*), 108

Pachycereus pringlei (cardons), 135

painted storks, 38

Pakhui Wildlife Sanctuary, 220

pale-billed woodpeckers, 55

Palicouria sp., 170

palms, 150, 160, 162

palm tanagers, 160, 169

palo santo trees (*Bursera grave-olens*), 62, 65–66

pampas zone, 62

Panajachel, Guatemala, 103–5

Panthera, 150

Papallacta, Ecuador, 171

paper mills, 71

papyrus reeds, 150

parakeets, austral, 13

paramo. *See* altiplano habitat

parasitic plants, 11

Parastrephia lepidophylla (tola), 113

parrots, 158–59

Pascura River, 14

Passiflora sp., 168

Patagonian forest, 9–12, 13–14

Path of the Panther Corridor (Mesoamerican Biological Corridor), 220

Patosia clandestine, 113

paujils (blue-billed curassows), 158–59

peacock butterflies, 208

peat bogs, 113

peccaries, collared, 127–28

pelicans, 27, 74, 95, 132

Penmon Point, 205, 206

Penmon Priory and Church, 206

Pensychnant, 209–10

peregrine falcons, 207

Populus trichocarpi (Alaskan black cottonwood), 187

porcelain orchid (*Chloraea magellanica*), 11–12

potatoes, 157

poverty

  in Guatemala, 111–12

  in India, 47, 53

  in Mexico, 137

  in Namibia, 139

Powers, Richard, 18–19

prairie, 18–19, 23

prairie chickens, 26–27

Prairie Dog Empire: A Saga of the Shortgrass Prairie (Johnsgard), 26

prairie dogs, 26

prairie restoration, 20

predator-prey interaction, 33, 34

Prentiss, Narcissa, 24

prickly pear cactus, 62, 119

prickly pear cactus trees (*Odonatus echios*), 66

prinias, 38

ProAves Foundation (Fundacion ProAves/Ecoturs), 155, 162–63

ProAves Women in Conservation program, 161, 162–63, 221

Pronatura Noroeste, 53

Prosopis ruscifolia, 110

protected lands. *See also* sanctuaries

  categories of, 3

  corridors for connecting, 220

  funding for, 220–22

  international, 4–5

  role of, 2, 217

  statistics on, 2

  successful, 218–22

  witnessing, 217

  writing about, 3–4

protective laws, 219

prothonotary warblers, 32

Protousnea sp., 11

Province of Pichincha, Ecuador, 169

ptarmigans, 185, 214

Puerto Ayora, Ecuador, 61–62, 63

Puerto Boyaca, Colombia, 157, 158

Puerto Pinzon, Colombia, 157

Puerto San Carlos, Mexico, 129, 135–37

Puffin Island, 206

puffins, 178, 188, 207

pufflegs, 170–71

pumas, 13–14

puna, 111–12, 114

puna flamingos, 114

restoration ecology, 204–5

Return to Warden's Grove: Science, Desire, and the Lives of Sparrows (Norment), 20–21

Revack estates, 213

rewilding, 204–5

Reykjavík, Iceland, 175, 176, 188

rhinoceros

    black, 140, 142

    one-horned Indian, 43–44

    white, 140, 142

Rhizophora mangles (red mangroves), 56

Rhodesian teak trees (*Baikiaea plurijuga*), 149

Rhodiola rosea (roseroot), 182–86

Rhododendron, 41, 168

Rhododendron alta, 41

Rhododendron arboretum, 41

Rice, Ann, 81

Ricketts, Ed, 131–32

ridge-crest habitat, 171

Rift Valley (Ethiopia), 89–90, 94–95

Rift Valley (Iceland), 186

Rimetea (Torocko), Romania, 85–86

ring road, 4, 178–79

Río Eléctrico, 3, 9–12, 13–14

riparian desert habitat, 122–25

Rivera, Juan, 103

Rivera, Maria, 103

road construction, 92–93

Road of Three Thousand Curves (Espinoza del Diablo), 52–54

roan antelope, 147

rock ptarmigans, 185

Rocky Mountain locust (*Melanoplus spretus*), 22–23

Rocky Mountains, 12–13, 119

Romania, 4, 81–86, 221

Roosevelt, Teddy, 167

Rose, Ananda, 120

roseroot (*Rhodiola rosea*), 182–86

rowan, 187

Royal Road (Camino Real Inca), 112

Royal Society for the Protection of Birds (RSPB), 203, 204–5, 206, 209, 213

rufous motmots, 161

rufous-tailed hummingbirds, 160, 167, 168

ruins

    Mayan, 4, 98, 99, 100

    military, 1, 25

Russell, Karen, 33

sable antelope, 142

Sahara desert, 1, 81

Sea of Cortez: A Leisurely Journal of Travel and Research (Steinbeck and Ricketts), 131–32

sea pink (*Armeria maritima*), 11

sea turtle nesting sites, 72

sedges, 62, 194, 198

sedge warblers, 194, 205

sensitive fern, 168

Seriol (saint), 206

Serrania de las Quinchas Mountains, 157

Sesuvium sp., 66

shade-grown coffee, 54

Shalhots, Iceland, 186

sharks, white-tipped reef, 66–67

shelducks, 205

Shelton, Richard, 119, 123

Shepard, Nan, 214

short-eared owls, 183–84

short grass prairie, 23

Showdown in the Sonoran Desert: Religion, Law and the Immigration Controversy (Rose), 120

shrimp aquaculture, 57

shrub magnolias, 72

Siberian jays, 195–96

Siberian larch (*Larix sukaczewii*), 187

Siberian pines (*Pinus sibirica*), 195

Siberian spruce (*Picea obovata*), 195

Siberian taiga, 195

Sierra Club, 123

Sierra de la Laguna Biosphere Reserve, 136–37

Sierra Laguna Mountains, 137

Sierra Madres, 51, 52–54, 59, 119, 221

Silene acaulis (moss campion), 178

silver-cluster leaf, 142–43

Simien fox. *See* Abyssinian wolf

Simien Mountains, 93

site of special scientific interest (SSSI), 206

Sitka spruce (*Picea sitchensen*), 187

sky islands, 4, 119–22

skylarks, 203

Slovanian grebes, 214

Smithy Cottage, 205

Snæfellsnes Peninsula, 176–77, 179

Snæfellsjökull National Park, 177

snipes, 184

Snowdonia National Park, 208–10

Snowdonia National Park Authority, 208

snowmelt, 39

snowy egrets, 32

snowy owls, 73

Solanum sp. (nightshade), 157

Sonora desert

Baja peninsula, 135

Chiricahua National Monument, 119, 120–21

dry tropical forest ecosystem, 137

peccaries in, 127–28

San Pedro River and, 122

South Africa, 140–41

southern beech (lenga) (*Nothofagus pumilio*), 10–11, 13, 15

South Plaza Island, 66–67

South Stack-RSPB Preserve, 206

Spanish moss, 71

sparkleberry, 71

sparrows

Bugun liocichla, 42, 43, 219

Harris's, 20–21

special protected area (SPA), 206

species distribution, 171

spectacled bears, 160

speleothems, 124

Spinnes Reserve, 206

Sprey River, 213

springs, La Tovara, 56, 57–58

spruce

Engelmann, 120

Norway, 187, 195

Siberian, 195

Sitka, 187

squirrel cuckoos, 98

SSSI (site of special scientific interest), 206

star frontlets, buff-winged, 170

St. Catherine's Church, 205

Steinbeck, John, 131–32

Stenocereus eruca (creeping devil cactus), 135

Stoker, Bram, 84

storks

greater adjutants, 45

marabou, 95

painted, 38

white, 71

wood, 32, 70–71

strangler figs, 51, 102, 159

Stykkishólmur, Iceland, 180

subalpine slopes, 10

sub-Himalayan forests, 39

sugarcane fields, 110

sumac, 126

sunbirds, 42

Suomala, Mark
  De Soto National Wildlife Refuge and, 20
  Fontenelle Forest and, 21
  on the high plains ecosystem, 23
  Iceland and, 176, 178–79, 180–81
  Omaha and, 19
  on prairie dogs, 25–26
sustainable farming, 54
swallows, 9, 148
Swamplandia (Russell), 33
swans, whooper, 183, 194–95
sweet flag (*Acorus calamus*) (Calamus), 27
Switzer, Bruce, 27–28
Switzer, Sue, 27–28
swordbill hummingbirds, 168, 170
sycamores, 120
Szekely Land, 82
tagua palm (*Phytelephas schottii* or *P. tenaicaulis*)., 162
taiga, Siberian, 195
tall grass prairie, 23
tanagers
  azure-rumped, 103
  blue and gray, 160
  crimson-backed, 160
  flame-faced, 169
  golden, 169
  lemon-rumped, 169
  palm, 160, 169
  scarlet, 157
  in Tikal, 99
Tandayapa Lodge, 168
Tandayapa Valley, 168
tawny owls, 214
Taxus baccata (yew), 82
Taylor Ranch, 27
teals, 206
tea plantations, 44, 45
Tehuelche language, 9
Tell Me a Riddle (Olsen), 28
temples, Mayan, 99, 100
Tepes, Vlad, 82, 84–85
terns, arctic, 185
terrorist groups, 109
tetrafluromethane, 189
Texas, 119–22, 126–28
thick-billed murres, 178
thicket birds, 131
Thingvellir Lake, 186
Thingvellir National Park, 177, 186
This Cold Heaven: Seven Seasons in Greenland (Ehrlick), 183

Twin Craters (Los Gemelos), 61

Typha angusatata, 38

tyrants, toady, 160

UNEP-WCMC (United Nations Environmental Programme World Conservation Monitoring Center), 2

UNESCO Biosphere Reserves, 57, 98, 113, 134

UNESCO World Heritage Sites

Galapagos Islands, 63, 221

Isla Espiritu Santos, 134

Kaziranga National Park, 44

Los Glaciers National Park, 14–15

Thingvellir National Park, 177

Tikal, 98

Torocko village, 85–86

Victoria Falls, 150–51

United Nations Environmental Programme World Conservation Monitoring Center (UNEP-WCMC), 2

United States. *See also* Arizona

Alabama, 4, 31–35

Amelia Island, 4, 69, 70–74

Nebraska, 17–29

New Mexico, 4, 119–22, 123–26

southwestern deserts of, 119–28

Texas, 119–22, 126–28

Ural owls, 82, 196

Urasian wedgens, 214

Urho Kekkonen National Park, 196

Urrea, Luis Alberto, 120

Ursus sp., 83–84

U.S. Army Corps of Engineers, 32

U.S. Bureau of Land Management, 123

U.S. National Wildlife Refuge system, 220

Usnea sp. (old man's beard), 11

utilitarian conservationism, 218

Vampire God: The Allure of the Undead in Western Culture (Hallab), 85

vampire mythology, 81, 82, 84–85, 86

Varanger Peninsula, 194, 197–98

Varanger Peninsula National Park, 198

Vatnajökull glacier, 177, 188–89

Vatnajökull National Park, 177

veldt, bush or thorn shrub, 139

verdins, 130

Verghese, Abraham, 95–96

vervet monkeys, 147

Vestmannaeyjar, Iceland, 175

Vík, Iceland, 188

Liminganlahti, 194

RAMSAR sites, 113

whales

fin, 178

gray, 4, 135–36

minke, 178

whaling, 177–78

Wheeler, Sara, 196

whimbrels, 183, 206

white-backed night herons, 147

white-faced capuchins, 160

white-faced nunbirds, 168

white fir, 120

White, Jim, 124

white mangroves (*Laguncularia racemosa*), 56

white-necked Jacobin hummingbirds, 160, 168

white pelicans, 27, 95

white rhinoceros, 140, 142

White River, 169

white storks, 71

white-tailed eagles, 183, 194

white-tipped reef sharks, 66–67

white-tipped sicklebill hummingbirds, 168

Whitney, Bill, 20

whooper swans, 183, 194–95

whooping cranes, 25

widgeons, 206

WildAid, 150

wild dogs, African, 150

wildebeest, blue, 142

wild syringe, 142–43

willows (*Salix* sp.), 144–45, 187, 198

willow warblers, 215

Wilson, E. O., 2–3, 151

Windhoek, Namibia, 139

Winllan woodlands, 211–12

wolves, Abyssinian, 4, 93–94, 219

Women in Conservation Program, 161, 162–63, 221

woodpeckers

cream-backed, 108

crimson-headed, 160

in eastern broadleaf forests, 41

flame-back, 40

imperial, 55

Magellanic, 13, 15

pale-billed, 55

pitio, 13

wood storks, 32, 70–71

wood thrushes, 215

wood warblers, 209

woody creepers, 102

World Commission on Protected Areas (WCPA), 2

Author Bio

Mary A. Hood is a retired professor of microbiology whose students have become contributing members of the community of U.S. microbiologists. Author of *The Strangler Fig and Other Tales: Field Notes of a Conservationist* (2004 Rowman & Littlefield), *River-Time: Ecotravels on the World's Rivers* (2008 SUNY Press), *Walking Seasonal Roads* (2012 Syracuse University Press), Mary has published a number of poetry collections, articles on conservation and the environment, and numerous scientific/technical articles in the field of microbial ecology. As a Bunting Fellow at Radcliffe Institute for Advanced Study, she worked at Harvard Medical School during the 80s, served as poet laureate for Pensacola, FL in the 90s and currently holds the title, Professor Emerita at the University of West Florida.

Made in the USA
Middletown, DE
07 June 2019